Invest NOW

THE PASSIVE APPROACH TO
WINNING WITH REAL ESTATE

Updated for 2023

Jim Pellerin

Invest NOW

Ordering Information:
Quantity sales. Special discounts are available on quantity purchases by corporations, associations, and others. For details, contact the "Special Sales Department" at the address above.

Invest NOW – The Passive Approach to Winning with Real Estate / Jim Pellerin. —1st ed.

Table of Contents

"Diversification is protection against ignorance. It makes little sense [to diversify] if you know what you are doing."

—WARREN BUFFET

Dedication

This book is dedicated to all the people who are interested in learning how they can develop a real estate-based investment strategy that will help them achieve their financial and retirement goals.

This book is dedicated to small business owners and professionals who are dedicated to their jobs and who haven't had the time to plan their investment strategies and who are currently looking for an alternative investment solution.

This book is dedicated to all those active real estate investors who have listened to the wrong advice and who want to learn other ways of making money in real estate using passive real estate investment strategies.

Preface

I have been involved in Real Estate Investing for over 25 years. I have learned a lot about Real Estate Investing during that time. I have made a lot of money and lost a lot of money as well. If I were to do it all over again, I would not have owned any real estate except for large apartment buildings.

Owning real estate has its fair share of responsibilities and liabilities. Most people do not make money from investing in real estate. Most people should not own real estate as an investment. To make money in real estate, you really need to know what you are doing. Almost everyone I know who has made money in real estate is doing it fulltime and have owned many properties.

The other books that I have written were instructional and were more focused on showing people how to get started in real estate investing and how to make money in real estate as an *active* real estate investor. This book, however, is the result of the many years of experience I have accumulated and is focused on how you can make money in real estate, *passively*, as opposed to exposing yourself to the challenges of direct ownership.

My new passion is to help people develop a real estate-based investment strategy that will effectively mature into a solid retirement fund that will provide an income stream for them when they retire.

What I find unforgivable is how our government and financial institutions have effectively brainwashed us into believing that most of us are being fully taken care of, all we have to do is take the advice of our investment advisors, and everything will be all right.

There are a lot of people out there still working who are in their 60's, 70's and 80's because they can't retire. Some of the people who fall within this age group have a large savings amount at their disposal. The problem is that these people don't often trust anyone with their money because our system has failed them.

This book shows you how you can get started in real estate investing the right way.

Chapter 1 will look at the psychology associated with having a good Investment Plan and demonstrates the need for having a strong WHY to help drive your plan.

Chapter 2 covers how important it is to break the procrastination cycle when it comes to saving and to start investing as soon as possible and to cut spending.

Chapter 3 analyzes the current financial situation and covers the problems that a lot of people are facing with respect to their retirement strategies and what they need to do to fix it.

Chapter 4 looks at traditional investing and covers some basic concepts so you will know what to look out for when seeking financial advice.

Chapter 5 introduces real estate as an alternative investment strategy and discusses many real estate investment strategies and the different ways to structure them.

Chapter 6 discusses being a passive investor since most people are too busy with their lives to acquire an adequate level of expertise to properly manage their own investments.

Chapter 7 looks at how you can make money by lending money to other people, just as if you were the bank. It also looks at how you can fund these loans.

Chapter 8 talks about Private Equity Investments and how they can serve as the ultimate passive real estate investment strategy, in comparison to other real estate investment strategies.

Chapter 9 helps you define a passive investment plan that is based on your overall goals and demonstrates ways in which you can diversify that plan.

Chapter 10 shows you how you can customize your passive investment plan using alternative investments and how you can use registered savings accounts as a vehicle to double and eventually triple your investment.

Canadian Content

The information covered in this book has been written from a Canadian perspective. This means we are referring to concepts and themes specific to the Canadian market and the governing systems of retirement and taxation. Specifically, we refer to Canadian retirement tax savings accounts and Canadian types of investment such as RRSPs and Private Equity investments.

However, all the concepts and ideas presented in this book can easily be applied to other geographical markets as well.

For example, RRSP references can be substituted for 401-Ks and IRAs in the United States. Private Equity investments are similar, but the focus is on real estate-based investments. Private mortgages are also similar across most markets.

The main concepts discussed in this book cover the underlying processes, rather than the distinct products that need to be acquired. We stress the importance of the decisions required to become a passive investor.

CHAPTER 1

Why You Need to Invest

In this chapter we will look at the power of WHY. The power of WHY is probably the biggest motivator for getting you to achieve your goals. You hear stories all the time about successful people who grew up poor and who never wanted to be without money again and who now want to enjoy the finer things in life. So, they drove themselves to be successful.

Other people want to be successful so they can help others in their time of need. They want to give back to their families and to their communities.

There's a popular story about two brothers. Their father was a criminal and was in and out jail all his life. One brother turned out to be very successful. When asked why he was so successful, he replied that he had no choice because of his father. The other brother was a criminal just like his father. When asked why he turned out that way, he replied that he had no choice because of his father.

Our WHY can motivate each of us in different ways.

There are 3 basic categories of "WHY you want to do something".

1. To Quit Your Job

Most people start something without ever knowing WHY they want to achieve their goal in the first place. Knowing your WHY can be a very powerful motivator. Knowing you WHY also helps you focus on your goals, knowing that, when you perform each task, it will bring you closer to your WHY.

If you are trying to build up your investment portfolio passively, you are going to have to earn your money from other sources. For some people, that may mean working at a job that they don't like. But knowing your WHY may make that job a little easier to deal with. Realistically, if you don't like your job I would encourage you to look for something else right away. But this is just an example of how knowing your WHY can help.

Maybe your investment strategy can bring you closer to finding a more enjoyable job that may pay less. But the earnings from your investments will make up the difference. Or maybe your investment strategy can give you more free time to spend with your family.

2. To Get You the Things You Want

Maybe your WHY is just you wanting to have some nice things that you currently cannot afford. Maybe you are working hard, saving money and investing it properly, because you are trying to save money for a cruise. That can be a powerful WHY. Or maybe owning your dream home is your ultimate WHY.

A lot of people are motivated by nice things. There's nothing wrong with that. The big problem with today's society is that people want instant gratification. They go into debt to buy the things that they want NOW, rather than saving and investing their money and waiting to earn the money required to buy those nice things. But the things that they buy will mean a lot more if they worked hard to earn the money to buy those things and if they didn't have to go into debt to get those things.

3. To Help Others

Another powerful WHY you might have is that you want to be able to have enough money to help others in their time of need. Like being able to put your kids through college. Most parents want a better life for their children and want to take care of them and make sure that their children have more opportunities than they had when they were growing up.

Most of us can expect that our own parents will need help later on in their life. We would be disappointed with ourselves if we were unable to help them.

There are lots of ways to help other people and there are a lot of emotional benefits gained from helping others when they need it the most.

1.1 - Why You Need a 'Why'?

TO REALLY GET INSPIRED TO DO SOMETHING OR TO ACHIEVE SOMETHING, YOU NEED A STRONG 'WHY'.

In Simon Sinek's book *"Start with Why"*, he talks about having your WHY at the center of what you want to accomplish. Once you have your 'WHY', then the 'WHAT' and the 'HOW' can be figured out a lot easier. You will be able to define what it is you are trying to achieve and what you need to do to achieve it. Finding your WHY will make everything you do a lot clearer and a lot more fun.

A lot of people hate their jobs, but they feel they need their jobs in order to survive. Having a job provides people with the income required to support their basic lifestyle which, according to Maslow's hierarchy, is the lowest level of human needs.

How do people end up in these unfulfilling jobs? At a young age, kids are taught to go to school, get a good education and then get a good job. You hear stories all the time about men and women working in their fields because their parents told them they had to go to university and become a lawyer or a doctor. These people do this only to find out years later that they are unfulfilled. And now they are stuck. They are stuck in a job they don't like, and they have no way of getting out. Some other people find out earlier than others that they hate their job and they decide from there on to start making changes. These people are the lucky ones.

And this applies to just about anyone, not just the people who were forced into a job that their parents picked for them. Most people get a job, and if it's a half-decent job. They end up staying in that job for the rest of their lives, or until they are fired, laid off or retire.

Getting laid off is even worse than quitting; because, now they are more desperate and have to find another job in a field, they have no interest in. In most cases, these people have to find a job right away because they have bills to pay. So, they end up taking the first job that comes along. And, if that job has a defined pension plan, then these people are even more motivated to stay and ride out the job for the long haul.

I was fortunate to have someone mentor me at a very young age. I was originally going to get a Physical Education degree. I didn't really know what kind of job I wanted; I just knew that I enjoyed sports. My Computer Science teacher talked me into getting a degree in Computer Science, which I really liked, and I ended up having a successful career in that field. To keep things interesting, I changed jobs about every 5 years, so I was never really tied down to any one job and I was always challenging myself with the next opportunity. Eventually, I became an independent consultant which was a whole different challenge.

If more people were encouraged to pursue a career in their field of interest, I think you would have a lot of happy people who have a stronger WHY with a more enjoyable life. But somehow their WHY got lost in their "need to" and "have to" approach to life.

"Life is what happens to you when you're busy making plans"

— John Lennon

Now, I'm not saying people can't be happy at their jobs. In fact, I have seen many people happy in a lot of different careers. However, I am convinced that those people have a strong WHY and that they are performing those jobs using their WHY as their main driver.

A strong WHY can provide motivation for you. It helps bring clarity to what you are doing whenever you are performing a task.

For example, good waiters and waitresses might think that their WHY is to provide their customers with happiness whenever they come to their restaurant. I have eaten at a lot of restaurants. It's obvious when your waiter or waitress has a bigger WHY than to just bring you your food and to get through their day so they can go home to their family and just crash on their couch and watch TV.

People with a stronger WHY have a stronger sense of purpose and a stronger sense of fulfillment and don't necessarily get burned out at the end of their workday. They go home feeling satisfied and still have lots of energy left to spend the rest of the day doing things with their families and friends.

The alternative is that some people get burned out doing something they don't like, or worse, something they hate. By the time these people get home, all they want to do is "relax". This is one reason why there are so many problems with addictions. People are looking for that escape from their current reality. People can get addicted to many things: food, alcohol, drugs, TV, video games, web surfing. All these things can be used to escape from a life that is unsatisfying, even if it's for only a moment.

If you have a strong WHY it will provide a lot of motivation. It will provide direction. It will provide clarity of purpose. It can make a boring job more exciting, more satisfying. It can also provide you with a sense of fulfillment, knowing that you are doing something that genuinely matters.

A strong 'WHY' should be at the center of your bigger plans and goals.

Once you have defined your WHY, then you can develop your action plan to achieve your goals. This plan is the "What" and the "How" that goes with your WHY. This can all start with something as simple as having a good investment plan.

If you have a sound investment strategy that is providing predictable results, it can also provide peace of mind knowing that you will be provided for. There are also significant health benefits to having a good investment plan.

Stress is a big contributor to bad health. Stress can cause you to eat poorly and become overweight. Stress can cause you to not sleep enough, and to not be able to exercise properly, because you are too tired, and you don't feel like it. It becomes a vicious circle.

Another important underlying cause of stress is debt. Not being able to pay your bills because you aren't making enough money or because you don't have a retirement plan can also cause a lot of stress because you think you might have to work for the rest of your life in order to survive. Gone are the days where an investment advisor is someone that helps you decide how and where you are going to invest your money. Now YOU have to decide where to invest your money.

Wouldn't it be nice knowing that every day when you go to work, you are providing the best service you can and making a difference, and at the same time contributing to a sound financial plan that will give you the financial freedom you want and that you deserve? A sound investment strategy may also give you the drive to accomplish more, knowing that there are options out there so you are able to look for more fulfilling work.

> ***Having a strong 'WHY' that is aligned with the goals and plans that you have for a better life, is the ultimate achievement.***

For example, wouldn't it be nice if you could perform as a musician and not have to worry about your finances because you have a passive investment strategy that is supplementing your income?

Having a strong WHY that is aligned with your goals and action plans will give you the ultimate confidence and power to make better choices in life and to enjoy life better. It will make you proud of your achievements and accomplishments.

So, let's define your WHY and develop the goals and plans around a sound passive investment strategy that will help you to achieve the results you are looking for.

1.2 - What Investing Can Do for You

There are many things that a good investment plan can do for you. Probably the biggest thing is that it provides you with a **choice**. The choice to do what you want and the freedom to do what you want.

A good investment plan can allow you to work at a job you **want** to work at, not at a job you **have** to work at. Too many people are working at jobs they don't like but feel they must, just so they can pay the bills. Look at how many people go to university, get a degree and then end up getting a job in a totally unrelated field.

A good investment plan can provide additional income. With this additional income, you can acquire some of the things you want. There are some basic fundamental needs that all people need, such as housing, clothing, food, healthcare, and shelter. But most people settle for the basics because that's all they think they can afford. They don't have a big enough WHY to motivate them.

Wouldn't it be nice to have an investment plan that generates a passive income stream that can help you buy a nice home or buy the car of your dreams or even purchase a cottage for you and your family to enjoy? Wouldn't it be nice to go out to nice dinners more often or to be able to afford fancy clothes? You only live once right?

But most people go into debt trying to upgrade their lifestyle so that it looks like they can afford that lifestyle. They are trying to "keep up with the Jones", as the old saying goes. It's called *conspicuous consumption*. The person next door gets a new car, so YOU have to get a new car.

As a result of this type of spending, there is more credit card debt now than ever before. And people are declaring bankruptcy a lot more these days. And just look at what happened in 2008 with the housing market crash. And still, most people are carrying way too much mortgage debt relative to their incomes, all because they want a nicer home that they can't really afford.

> ***Wouldn't it be nice to be able to afford a nicer home, knowing that your investment plan is paying for it, or at least helping to pay for it?***

Oh, and for you people who have paid off your home, you have dead equity in your home, and you should be using it in your overall investment strategy.

When I hear people tell me that they own their home free and clear and they don't have a mortgage, I say to them … "that's too bad". Your home is an asset and should be treated as such. You need to leverage the equity in your home for more investments. You might think this is risky? But not if you have the right investment plan, the right investment products, and the right investment advisor.

I had one investor I was speaking with who had purchased a couple of investment properties with cash and he was renting them out. Both these properties were earning him an income, which was covering his taxes and providing him with good cash flow. But the return on his investment was very low because all his cash was tied up in these 2 properties. He wasn't using leverage.

For example, assume you purchase a property for $100,000, with all cash. Next, assume your property increases in value by $10,000 and is now worth $110,000. You made a return of 10% on this investment (we will ignore rents and expenses in this example). Next, assume that you borrowed money to purchase the same property and you only had to put $20,000 down. Assume the property increases by 10% as well. Now the return on your investment is 50% instead of the 10% because you only had invested $20,000 and not

$100,000. A better solution for this investor might have been to invest the $100,000 to buy 5 properties with a $20,000 investment in each.

I put together a plan for the investor that would see him refinancing these two properties, purchasing another four properties, and increasing his positive cash flow to a total of $100,000. We are still discussing his options. The point is that most people need help with their investment plans.

> ***Another thing a good investment plan can provide is time. More time to spend with family. More time to take vacations when you want.***

For most people, a good investment plan can provide financial independence. A lot of people want the security of knowing they never have to work again because they have enough money saved up and those savings are generating enough income. This means their investments are providing for them so that they can actually retire from a job they hate.

I have a lot of friends who continue to work, not because they want to, but because they have to. Some of these people have saved a lot of money but they don't know where to invest it because they have no investment plan and they don't trust anyone to invest their money with. The investment plan they have been relying on has failed them. So, they continue to work without a plan.

The biggest problem today is that people have given up control of their investments and their investment planning to investment advisors. While these advisors may have good intentions for their clients, they just don't have the right products for their clients to invest in. These investments don't provide their clients with the returns they will need or the security they desire.

Most people these days do not have defined pension plans and they are left to try and create their own investment plan that will provide for them in retirement. They go see an investment advisor and that advisor will look at a bunch of mutual funds and recommend they spread their money over a few mutual funds to try and diversify their portfolio. These funds are still invested in only stocks and bonds, which isn't real diversification since they are just investing in the same asset class. A lot of people have lost a lot of money in the stock market by investing this way.

So, what do the advisors tell their clients when their investments are down in value? *"Oh, the markets are set to recover soon"*. Meanwhile, these poor people are sitting on a portfolio that is worth half as much as what they started with and now they may have to work for the rest of their lives to recover from these losses. And for most people, this is not an option since their jobs have a mandatory retirement age and their health will not let them work that long. You are seeing a lot of elderly people working at fast-food restaurants these days, which has a bad impact on the whole job market and the overall economy.

So, what happens when these people can no longer work? Their children end up having to take care of them or the government will have to subsidize them longer. People are living a lot longer than what was originally planned when the retirement age was supposed to be 65. And people are running out of money before they die. It's not a good situation.

A good investment plan must provide long-term security for you.

It must provide security knowing that you can retire; that you will be taken care of in your golden years; that you will have a predictable income for many years to come and that you won't have to rely on your children or the government to get you through your final years.

1.3 - What Investing Can Do for Others

Another thing to think about when deciding your WHY, is to think about what your investments can do for others? Maybe you want a good investment plan so that you can help provide for others in their time of need. How can your investment plan help your friends and family? This is usually the strongest WHY that people have when they define their WHY.

A lot of people are investing so that they can leave something behind for their children. Of course, this is only after they have provided for themselves. Parents want better things for their children and want to give them a helping hand. And maybe that helping hand happens while they are still alive.

An investor friend of mine just told me that the money he made from his last investment with me will be given to his daughter to help her out with the down payment on her new home.

> ***Wouldn't it be nice knowing that you can help your kids as they start their own life?***

Another way you can help your kids is to pay for their university education. University and college education are very expensive, and most families can't afford to send their kids to university. So, what happens is they have to arrange for a student loan. And these loans come with a high interest rate. Student loans are usually prime +5%. Another option is to apply for a grant or a bursary. Both of which are never guaranteed and are very specific and hard to get. Wouldn't it be nice to pay for your child's education, knowing they can start their life free of any debt?

And what if your child got sick or was in an accident and needed some type of emergency health care? Wouldn't you want to help? Medical expenses are getting more and more expensive and a lot of people don't have a medical plan to help insure themselves against unexpected problems.

And what if one of your children lost their job suddenly? Wouldn't it be nice to be able to help?

Now, I'm not saying you want your children to be dependent on you in their adult years. You certainly want them to grow up to be responsible adults. I am just suggesting that sometimes people need a helping hand to get them through some serious unplanned event and it's nice to be able to help when they need it.

And this help doesn't have to apply to just your children. It could mean helping other family members and close friends as well.

At the other end of life, your parents may need your help. Specialized homes can be very expensive and the level of care can be much different depending on the price of the facility. Generally, the more expensive the facility, the better the care. And drugs are very expensive if they don't have proper medical insurance. Wouldn't it be nice to be able to help your parents when they get older so that they can receive the care they deserve?

Also, by showing that you care for your family, you are setting an example for your own children. They may better position themselves so that they can take care of you when you get older. And your children would also help their own children if they needed their education paid for or help with their down payment on their home. By setting an example, you are instilling the practice in your children to establish a good investment plan as well.

Another thing people like to do is to donate to their favorite charity. Having a good investment plan can allow you to contribute and make donations to a worthwhile cause of your choice. Having a good investment plan can allow you to spend more time and money on your favorite charity. Do you have a worthwhile cause that you would like to help with, from a financial perspective, and from a time commitment perspective? If not, it's probably because you can't afford one. Most successful people are donating some time and money to their favorite charity and to their children.

Another thing you can do with a good investment plan is you can give back to your community. Because you have a sound financial plan and financial freedom, you are able to spend more time with your community. You can join a local club and volunteer your time and money. For example, some people would spend more time with their church, if they could afford to.

Maybe you have someone you know, or a family member, looking to start up a new business? Or someone who needs help with their existing business. Getting business loans can be difficult. With a good investment plan, you might have the freedom to invest in this business. Not only are you helping someone out, but you might also benefit from this in the form of a good return on your investment. But you have to be clear with yourself that this is a donation and not an investment and that you are not expecting to make any money from the deal. But you probably don't want to communicate your contribution this way to the person you are investing with.

> ***People who get a "donation" for their business may not be as motivated to be successful.***

People who borrow money from friends and family are very motivated to succeed because they don't want to let those people down and they don't want to be embarrassed when they see these people at social gatherings.

There's an old saying that you should never lend money to friends and family because of the possibility that you might lose your investment and ruin your friendship or alienate family members. So, you must enter into this type of business venture knowing that it is simply a donation, rather than an investment. Certainly, there is a time where you would invest with an expectation that you would make a return on your investment, but this is not what I am referring to here. This is about helping others succeed because you have the ability to, and because you had the foresight to start a good investment plan.

As you can see, there are lots of ways a good investment plan can be used to help others. It's not just about doing something for yourself. Certainly, you want to make sure that you are financially sound, but then what you do after that can be very satisfying.

In conclusion, a good investment plan can be used for many different things. But be careful, when investing in others. People may want to take advantage of your generosity.

CHAPTER 2

How to Invest NOW

In this chapter, we will show you why it's important to start to invest NOW. I hear people say all the time that NOW is not the right time to invest. That's a bunch of crap. These same people are always waiting for the right time to invest. But when is the right time to invest?

> ***NOW is always the right time to invest, as long as you invest in the right thing and as long as you know what you are doing.***

The earlier you start to invest, the less that you will have to invest over time to make the same amount of money. This is because of the power of compound interest.

It's like the story of the tortoise and the hare.

The hare starts out fast and it looks like he is going to win the race. But eventually, he gets tired and has to lie down. The tortoise, on the other hand, starts out slow and stays slow but moves consistently at the same pace the whole race. Eventually, the tortoise passes the hare and wins the race.

> ***Slow and steady wins the race.***

In real estate, a lot of people are looking for the "get rich quick" path. Therefore, they are sucked into some of these highly speculative ventures or they start buying real estate and have no idea what they are doing. They choose the wrong real estate investment strategy because they are listening to other people who have totally different goals than they have.

The get rich quick investor is an example of the "hare" approach to investing in real estate. Over time, they realize that they haven't made any money because their costs exceeded their income and equity growth. And they have lost a lot of money because they didn't know what they were doing and they didn't take the time to learn or to find someone to work with, that does know what they are doing.

Then you have the "tortoise" real estate investor.

First, they define their goals, so that they are clear what they are looking for. And these goals are aligned with their WHY. Next, they figure out which investment strategy makes sense for them. Then they start executing that strategy. They start building their investment portfolio at an early age.

For example, someone who started investing at age 25 with $7,000 and contributed another $7,000 every year until they reach 65, would have grown their portfolio to $3.4M. Someone who waited until they were 45, and invested an initial $200,000 and continued to contribute $25,000 each year until they were 65, would have only grown their portfolio to $3.1M.

The person who started late would have invested $700,000 compared to the person who started at age 25 who would have only had to contribute $287,000. That's a big difference. This example assumes a 10% return and the investment was with funds from a registered tax savings account.

> ***Starting to invest as soon as possible also helps builds a habit.***

People need to set up a savings program where they take a certain amount of their income and set it aside each month. Investing on a regular basis builds a habit and builds confidence. There is currently a spending epidemic in North America.

> ***People use their credit cards to buy things they don't need with money they don't have and end up making payments they can't afford.***

You also want to make sure that your investment will beat inflation. This means that you need to find good investments that provide a good return that exceeds the annual inflation rate, at the very least. A good real estate investment should provide a minimum of 8% return.

You will also need to define, or redefine, who you are. You need to transform yourself from a non-investor, who spends all of their money, into a smart investor, who saves and invests a lot of their money.

2.1 - Why You Need to Invest Now

Why do you need to invest now? Because time equals money. Lost time equals lost money.

The longer you wait to invest, the more opportunity you lose to make money, so the less money you will make. Time is money.

Millions of people have lost money in their investments. Over the past 10 years or more the stock market has underperformed. Mutual funds and bonds are at an all-time low. Savings account interest rates are laughable. Many people who have invested in real estate have lost money.

People are scared and they don't know what to do.

How are people going to retire? They think that they are going to have to work forever … or at least until they die.

Waiting for things to change is not the answer either. Especially in today's volatile market. Stock prices are easily influenced by events outside of your control. So, what do risk-averse people do? They do nothing. They think that the safest thing to do is keep their "nest egg" safe by not investing in anything.

The best thing to do in this case is to look for alternatives.

Part of the problem is that most people have been relying on "experts" to manage their investments for them and they have no idea what to do now. These experts are licensed to deal in securities and to push the products they are authorized to sell. For example, a stockbroker cannot sell real estate investments. They can only sell securities such as stocks and bonds. Mortgage brokers are not licensed to sell stocks and bonds. They can only sell mortgage investments.

There's an old saying: *"If you're a hammer, everything looks like a nail"*. If you go to a stockbroker, they will sell you stocks. Go to real estate investor and they will sell you real estate investments.

But here's the real problem:

> ***If you don't invest your money...you are actually losing money!***

Inflation will eat away at your savings.

Inflation (as defined in Investopedia)

> *Inflation is defined as a sustained increase in the general level of prices for goods and services. It is measured as an annual percentage increase. As inflation rises, every dollar you own buys a smaller percentage of a good or service.*

The following information shows the year-end inflation for Canada and the USA from 2008 to 2016.

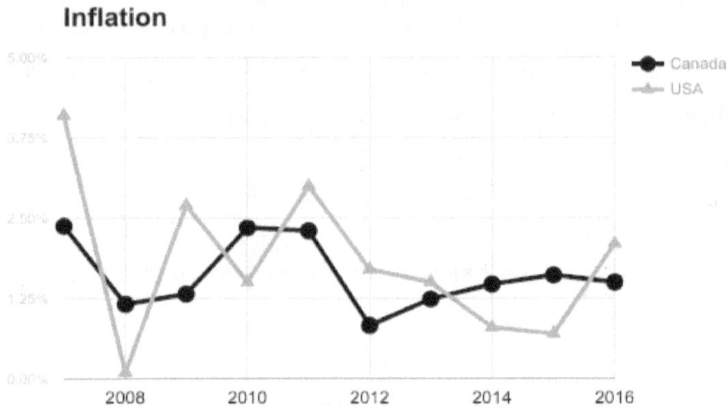

	2007	2008	2009	2010	2011	2012	2013	2014	2015	2016
Canada	2.38	1.16	1.32	2.35	2.30	0.83	1.24	1.47	1.61	1.50
USA	4.10	0.10	2.70	1.50	3.00	1.70	1.50	0.80	0.70	2.10

In the 10 years from 2006 to 2016, the dollar has lost about 15¢ in value as shown in the chart below. What's interesting is that both Canada and the USA have had very similar inflation rates.

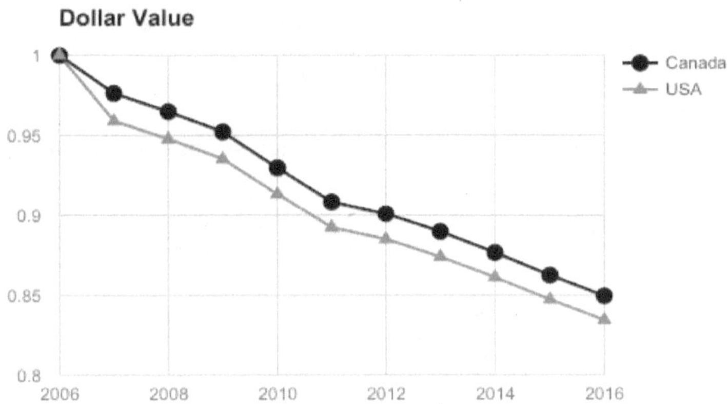

	2006	2007	2008	2009	2010	2011	2012	2013	2014	2015	2016
Canada	1.00	0.98	0.96	0.95	0.93	0.91	0.90	0.89	0.88	0.86	0.85
USA	1.00	0.96	0.95	0.94	0.91	0.89	0.88	0.87	0.86	0.85	0.83

Now you can only buy 8.50 widgets with your $1.00 because your dollar is worth 15¢ less after 10 years.

Opportunity Costs

The other big thing to be concerned about is the lost *opportunity cost* of not Investing that money NOW.

The more time you take in deciding what to invest in, the more money you lose. That lost money is your lost opportunity cost while your money is sitting in your savings account earning 1% or less per year.

For example, let's say there is an investment opportunity that you are looking at that pays 12%. Investments like this in real estate are more common than you think. You just need to look for them and you need to know where to find them. As of the time of this writing (2017), I have investment opportunities available that are currently paying 8%, 10%, and 15%. Each opportunity comes with different risks and different security.

Now, assume you have $100,000 sitting in a savings account that is currently not being invested in anything. Each month you delay your decision to invest costs you $1,000. ($100,000 x 12% = $12,000 / 12 months = $1,000 per month).

> ***I'm not suggesting you go out and invest in any new opportunity tomorrow just so you can get your money working faster.***

What I am suggesting is that you start educating yourself on these alternative types of investments so you can start making intelligent decisions.

It's time to take back control of your financial situation. People have had it easy for too long. They have relied on other people who have no control over the investment products they are selling you. There is not much you can do if a company's stock drops all of sudden, just because the price of oil has increased, and the company's operational costs have increased. The shock factor stemming from the results of an election, for example, could very well influence the stock price — causing your investment to drop by 50% or more!

> ***For the most part, stock prices are affected by the expectation of an event and not the actual event itself. It's about perception.***

Investing is gambling. Pure and simple. You can reduce your risk and increase your chances of winning by investing in the right products from people who have the right knowledge — the real experts. You need to let the pros do the work for you. I'm not talking about stockbrokers who have no influence over the performance of a company. I'm talking specifically about people who are closer to the product you are investing in … the real hands-on people! In the case of real estate investing, I'm referring to investors, developers, builders, etc.

I had one project where I was developing 15 townhomes. I had several investors involved in the deal. The project was stalled due to delays in the land approval process. My builder called me and said he had an opportunity to buy another piece of land close by. We ended up moving the project to that land and we were able to start building within the month. That's what happens when you are dealing with someone that is experienced and can influence the outcome of a particular project.

> ***Waiting for the market to turn around is not the right thing to do. The right thing to do is look for alternatives so you can Invest Now.***

Like the old saying goes: *'Nothing ventured, nothing gained'*.

You might as well let the experts do all the hard work for you. Check out the investment opportunities that are available to you from experienced people.

There are many good investments available today if you pay close attention and look for them. You just have to take back control of your situation and take your retirement planning seriously.

2.2 - Save NOW

The first thing you need to do before you can Invest NOW is to Save NOW.

There is a saying in time management that says, "the amount of time *required* to do a specific job will expand to the amount of time *available* to do that job". So, if you have 1 week to get a task completed, you will take a week. If you only have 2 days to complete the same task, you will figure out how to complete that task within 2 days, if it's important enough.

The same type of principle applies to savings, spending and investing.

> ***The amount of money spent on disposable items will increase as the amount of disposable income available increases.***

Basically, it means, the more money you make, the more money you will spend on disposable items. Disposable items are things that are nice to have but not things that you really need. These are the fun things.

There is a real epidemic in North America related to overspending.

People are looking for instant gratification. People are looking for the latest gadgets. Look at the lineups at the Apple store when they announce the latest iPhone. And half of those people are young adults living in their parents' basement.

Some people want to own the nicest and best cars. Some people want to own the most expensive house they can afford. Why? It's all about conspicuous consumption. This is something I learned about back in Grade 12 economics (NOTE: That was many, many years ago).

Some people want other people to think they can afford all these luxuries. Keeping up with the "Jones" as it used to be called … and maybe still is. That was the way a lot of people thought. The person next door got a new car so you had to get a new car. To have a successful savings and investing plan, this type of thinking must stop. At least, not until you have reached your investment goals and you can pay for these things the right way.

> ***If you have to "charge" something on your credit card because you can't afford to pay cash for it, then you can't afford to buy it. It's that simple.***

Credit cards should only be used as a convenience, not as a loan. But banks have made it easier and easier to get credit. It constantly amazes me when people come into my office and they tell me they have $30K or $40K or $50K of credit card debt. And they are driving a brand-new top of the line truck that they bought for $70K … on credit. Their justification is that *"you only live once"*. I have never purchased a new car and I always drive my cars until the repairs get too expensive to justify owning it. Right now, my car is 10 years old.

The other thing that always amazes me is when I meet with people and they tell me they have $20K in savings and then I find out they are carrying huge amounts of credit card debt that actually exceeds their savings? We are a debt society and we have lost perspective.

> ***The problem is that the more debt people carry, the fewer funds they can direct toward their savings and investments.***

Look at the following news announcements from Statistics Canada.

> *In 1980, the ratio of household debt to personal disposable income was 66%; that ratio recently passed the 150% figure). This means that, in aggregate, households owed more than $1.50 for every dollar of disposable income. Household debt is, therefore, an increasingly important component of the finances of many Canadian families.*
>
> Source: Statistics Canada, 2011
>
> *Statistics Canada said Wednesday the ratio of household credit market debt to adjusted disposable income crept up to 166.9 percent in the third quarter, up from 166.4 percent in the second quarter. That means, on average,*

Canadians owed $1.67 in credit market debt — mortgages, other loans, and consumer credit — for every dollar of disposable income.

Source: Statistics Canada, 2016

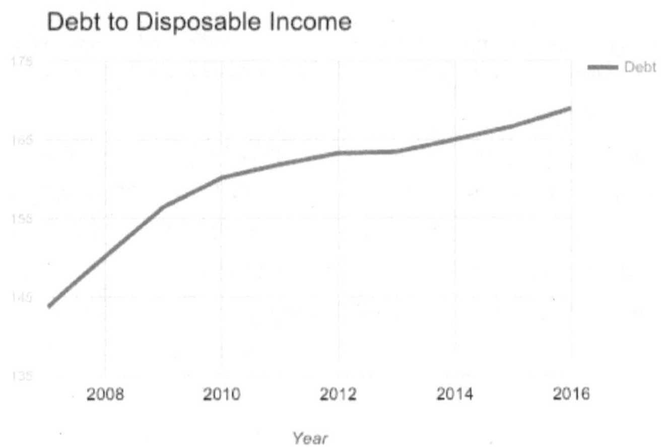

But all this spending comes at a price. Previously, I wrote about the lost opportunity cost. The more you spend on disposable items, the less you have to invest and the more opportunity you have lost to invest in good investment products and to earn a passive income.

For a lot of people, this is becoming a big problem. The closer you get to retirement age, the more concerned you become about having to work for the rest of your life. I hear people tell me all the time that they don't know how to retire. I saw a post on Facebook the other day where someone said he would be working until about noon on the day of his funeral.

This attitude towards debt and a lack of savings is not something to joke about.

But we North Americans always find ways to make fun of our situation. It somehow seems to make it OK if we can joke about it. And besides, everyone else they know is in the same situation. "Misery loves company", as the saying goes.

But what if you can't work much longer? What if you have unexpected health problems? What if the job you have or the industry you are in is becoming obsolete? As society develops, as technology develops, it changes the way people do things. Look at what has happened to the newspaper industry … or even the print industry in general. People are using their phones now for just about everything. I use my phone to call people, text people, email people, take notes, check my calendar, take pictures, record videos, live stream events, connect my computer to the internet, read everything I need to read and do research online.

I can basically run my business from my car and all I need is my laptop and my phone. They have even come out with a mini projector that attaches to your phone so I could be ready to do a presentation within a moment's notice.

The good news is that the majority of debt payments are going towards mortgage payments. What that means is you have more money to invest than you think.

People are richer than they think.

I hear people tell me all the time that their mortgage is paid off, or it's almost paid off. Yet, those same people are carrying debt on their credit cards. How does carrying $30,000 worth of credit card debt at 20% make sense when they could pay that debt off by using some of the equity in their house and only have to pay 3.5% on a Home Equity Line of Credit. The problem is that people don't understand this concept because they haven't taken the time to educate themselves.

The other thing people could do with the equity in their home is to use it to invest in high yield investments. Borrow at 3.5% and invest at 10%. Again, people haven't taken the time to educate themselves.

So, when people tell me their mortgage is almost paid off, I tell them *"that's too bad"*. People are obsessed with paying down their mortgage to provide, what they call, financial freedom. They think that once their mortgage is paid off they can live off their old age security and whatever other income benefits they might have. They are paying down their mortgage that only costs them 2.5%, increasing their debt, which costs them 20%, and not saving or investing which could actually generate a return that could contribute to their long-term savings and investments.

> ***What people need to do NOW is practice discipline and look at short term pain for long term gain and avoid this instant gratification, quick-fix mentality.***

The first thing I do when I sit down with people is I look at how much savings they have, how much equity is in their homes and the amount of debt they have built up. Then I develop a debt elimination and long-term savings and investment strategy for them.

Here's a typical example of something most people can do if they just take the time to educate themselves and find the right experts to help them.

Let's say John comes to me and he has $100,000 of available equity in his home and about $50,000 worth of debt in credit cards and whatever other loans he has. He also has about $100,000 room in his RRSP because he has never contributed to it. What a waste.

I would map out a plan whereby John would set-up an equity line of credit for $100,000. He would immediately pay off his $50,000 debt. That would provide him with about $1.500 a month that he could start saving instead of paying the same amount on his credit cards each month. 3% which is usually the minimum monthly payment required for credit cards. That's $18,000 per year savings (minus the line of credit payments) instead of debt repayment.

Then I would instruct John to put the other $50,000 in his RRSP. I would then place his RRSP in a self-directed real estate investment at 10%, which would earn him $5,000 a year. Assuming his Line of Credit (LOC) interest rate is only

2.5%, John would only be paying $2,500 a year on the LOC so he would be netting $2,500 overall on his investment.

The other big benefit is that John would receive a $20,000 tax rebate or tax reduction because of the RRSP tax reduction (assuming a 40% marginal tax rate). He would then deposit that $20,000 into his RRSP account and we would also invest that into another 10% investment.

John now has $70,000 invested that is earning him $7,000 per year minus $2,500 interest on the LOC loan. He would also have an extra $18,000 savings from the elimination of the credit card debt payment. His net worth has also increased by $20,000 and continues to increase at $4,500 ($7,000 - $2,500) plus the $18,000 per year if he continues to focus on a savings and investment strategy.

> ***The big change that must happen is a mindset change. The focus must be on Investing and Saving.***

You need to go from *Spend NOW* to *Save NOW* to *Invest NOW.*

2.3 - Who You Need to Become

Part of developing a good saving and investing strategy is changing who you are and the way you think about investing. You need to change your mindset.

There are several reasons why you may not have your investments in order and why you don't have a good investment strategy. People usually fall into one of the following types of investors.

The Non-Investor: Spending NOW

A lot of people are distracted by wanting the "finer" things in life and are caught up with trying to buy things they don't really need. They are simply satisfying their spending addiction. And for some people, it is an addiction. I have even heard the term "retail therapy". These people want the immediate gratification they get from spending and buying things for themselves.

Instead of saving for the future, some people are Spending NOW and they have spent way too much money on "stuff" they don't really need. Not only have they spent too much money on things they don't really need, but they have also borrowed money to purchase these things. This is why there is such a large amount of personal debt in our country.

People in this situation usually know they have done something wrong and feel very badly about where they are financially and feel they have no way out. These people need the most help.

The Misguided Investor: No control Over Your Finances

The Misguided Investor has put their investments into the hands of the wrong people. They have followed the typical investment strategy and have listened to their investment advisors. Investment advisors who make recommendations to people and get them to put their hard-earned money into investments that they have no control over.

Remember, licensed investment advisors are usually only licensed to make recommendations for certain types of investments. Stockbrokers can recommend investing in stocks and bonds but cannot recommend other types of investments, such as real estate. The only type of diversification they can provide is getting you to invest in different stocks and bonds.

People in this situation are upset with their advisors and are angry about the fact that they have not taken better control of their own savings and investments. It's time to take back control of their investments and their life.

The Busy Investor: Investing in the Wrong Investments

The Busy Investor has taken control of their investments, or at least they think they have taken control of their investments.

They no longer use a financial advisor. They are managing their own investments by buying and selling stocks themselves. They do their own research and make their own investment choices. The challenge with this approach is that they still have no control over the product they are investing in and they have no way to influence the success of your investment or the company they have invested in.

The bigger challenge is that you can't ever become an expert in the company you are investing in. How can you analyze all the things you need to analyze so that you can make an intelligent investment decision? Some companies have 100-page documents describing their products, operations, and financial situation. And it only takes an unrelated external event to influence the company's performance and you, the investor, have no control over that event or its effect.

People in this situation are frustrated and tired of trying to figure it out. They have spent many hours trying to analyze everything they can about the company. This strategy is not sustainable and has a very low chance of success. It's time to look to experts, with the right investments, so you can have more control over your investments.

The Disgruntled Investor: Someone Who Doesn't Know What to Invest In

The Disgruntled Investor has figured out that they need to take back control of their investments and they have fired their investment advisors. This usually happens after they have suffered a massive loss and they are trying to figure out how to recover from their losses.

These people realize that the investments they have been investing in are highly volatile and they aren't comfortable having so much uncertainty in their investment strategy. These people don't have much time to spend analyzing the investments themselves. Instead, their money is sitting in a savings account while they look for a safe investment, that provides a good rate of return. The problem is that they have started looking for a good investment strategy but they haven't found one and they don't know what to do.

So, they start looking at real estate and end up buying the wrong kind of real estate investment for them. They buy a home and rent it out thinking that it will provide them with some type of positive cash flow. These people are very busy and don't have the time to be a landlord. They have listened to the so-called real estate experts. But they still have a large amount of money they can't invest. They need to find properties, find tenants, get approved for financing and manage the properties.

People in this situation are usually disgruntled real estate investors because they are busy landlords and they don't have a lot of time to do all that needs to be done to manage their properties properly. I have quite a few clients like this that are now looking for passive investments.

The Smart Investor: Taking Control and Investing Smart

The Smart Investor seeks out the help of experts who can provide the right investments for them. These experts will also manage investments for them. These investments provide a good return and require no involvement from the investor, other than when it's time to reinvest. These are truly passive investments.

The real *expert* also assists the investor is laying out an overall plan for the investor and looks at all aspects of their financial situation. They aren't just trying to sell them the product of the day. They provide more of an advisor perspective.

Smart Investors are excited. They are very happy about what they are doing. They have a plan for the future. They are OK with giving up their instant gratification habits. They are OK that they aren't keeping up with the Jones. They are proud that they are making good sound investments in the products they are investing in.

These investors will even become a supporter and a spokesperson for the product and service.

The whole conspicuous consumption thing is usually about keeping up with the Jones and trying to outspend and out-purchase the neighbor or friend. People want to "show off" their latest purchase or their latest new car for example. But what about showing off your new investment strategy. Wouldn't it be cool if you were able to talk to people about your latest investment strategy? *"I am investing in this new condo development". "I have this new investment that's earning me a 10% consistent return year after year."*

At first, people will resent you for having taken control of your investments and for taking the necessary action that you needed to take. A lot of times these other people are just like you are … or were. They have tons of debt, lots of nice stuff, but no savings and investment strategy. But eventually, you will find

1 or 2 people who will put their jealousy aside and ask you for more information. They are still trying to keep up with the Jones, but instead of buying the flashy things, they are investing in their future … just like you. You are building a tribe of like-minded investors.

Your goal is to become a raving fan of your investment strategy.

Become obsessed with your savings and your investment strategy. It's very motivating and very fulfilling to know that you now have a solution that you are in control of.

Save NOW → Invest NOW

IF YOU WOULD LIKE MORE INFORMATION ON OUR PROGRAMS AND HOW WE MIGHT BE ABLE TO HELP, CHECK OUT THIS WEBSITE: **WWW.JIMPELLERIN.COM**

CHAPTER 3

The Current Situation

In this chapter, we will be discussing the current situation of some people's investments and how people have been misled. A lot of people are looking for the right investment strategy. They have been told to listen to their investment advisor and to invest their money into mutual funds.

The problem with this approach is that most of these recommendations are not able to help people grow their portfolios so that they can retire when they want to. These investments are too volatile and the returns they are providing are too low.

Let's look at an example:

Bill is a 25-year-old Business Analyst and starts working for ABC Corp. He is told that if he contributes to his RRSP account, ABC Corp would match his contribution, and all this can be set up so it happens automatically. Bill isn't sure what all this means, but he likes the idea of saving for retirement, especially if the company is matching his contribution. Next, Bill meets with the Human Resources department, fills out the necessary forms, and agrees to contribute a specific amount every month.

The next thing Bill has to do is set up an appointment with an Investment Advisor with the investment firm that ABC Corp has partnered with, so he can decide where to invest his RRSP funds. So, Bill meets with John, an Investment Advisor with The Right Time Investments Corp (RTIC).

John recommends that Bill invest his money in 2 Mutual Funds. Since Bill is still young, John recommends an aggressive fund and a balanced fund. John recommends an asset mix with some different types of companies. Bill is not sure what John is talking about but he agrees to these investments. He trusts John since John is a Senior Analyst with RTIC and has lots of initials after his name so he must know what he is talking about. Bill assumes that John has put together a plan that will make sure Bill has enough money to retire with.

Does this sound familiar? The problem with this strategy is that Bill has absolutely no control over what his investments are and how they are performing. And all his investments are in stocks and bonds. And because the investments are in mutual funds, it appears that his portfolio is diversified.

It's now 30 years later, Bill looks at his portfolio and he doesn't have hardly enough money to retire. He was hoping to retire at 55. Now he starts looking for other better performing investments. He has heard real estate is a good way to make money so he starts buying some real estate because he needs to make some money fast.

The problem with this typical story is that Bill was never in charge of his investment strategy. He relied on other people, such as his investment advisor, to make decisions and recommendations. He didn't take the time to learn more about his investments and he left it up to people he didn't know, hoping they had his best interest in mind.

3.1 - Help ... I Can't Retire

Are you one of the many people who is stuck without a retirement solution?

More and more people are finding themselves in this situation. They did everything they thought they had to do, but somehow society has let them down. They got tricked into thinking that someone was looking out for them and their financial future. They let their financial advisors make all the decisions for them.

Many people gave up financial control to their financial planners, mutual fund dealers, bankers, etc. All of these professionals are licensed to provide financial advice to people who seek it. In reality, these planners are nothing but glorified salespeople who are just trying to get you to invest your money with them so they can get paid by making a commission on the investments you make.

Now don't get me wrong. There are some people who do care about you and there are some people who are very good at what they do. But the big problem is that these people have no control over the products they are recommending that you invest in. Personally, I have never liked the stock market.

> ***As far as I'm concerned, the stock market is just a big casino where there are many ways to gamble and lose your money.***

Yet the stock market is legal because the people who are giving you advice and the people you are giving your money to are licensed.

These investment advisors are not intentionally trying to screw you over. Most of them have good intentions. The problem is that these advisors are selling you something that is very volatile and that you have no control over. For instance, what if you had invested a lot of money in Google and suddenly there's a big announcement stating that there's a new competitive search engine on the market that is going to kill Google?

Just this news and the thought of something happening to a company could have an immediate negative effect on the stock price and your investment along with it.

The big problem, in this situation, is that there's nothing you can do about it except hope that the stock rebounds to recover your losses or that the stock prices rise back to a profitable level.

At least with a good Real Estate investment, there are always a lot of things you can do to offset any bad situation.

- There are many ways to force appreciation
- There are many exit strategies that you can take
- There are ways to repurpose your property

Real estate has outperformed every other investment year after year.

On average, the median house price in Canada has increased by approximately 11.7% per year for the last 15 years.

Some people have a government or company pension plan. But a lot of people don't have a defined pension plan. Many companies have stopped providing a corporate pension plan and are just simply contributing to people's RRSPs and letting people manage their own retirement plans themselves.

The problem with letting people manage their own RRSP retirement plan is that people don't really know how to manage a stock portfolio or a mutual fund investment.

Most people have been relying on their banks to manage their RRSP accounts. And most banks have been investing those accounts into the bank's own mutual fund investments.

There are two serious problems with letting banks manage your retirement accounts.

1. The people handling your investment accounts are very biased. They are very motivated (usually through commissions) to place your hard-earned money into their own mutual funds or other investment products.

2. The stock market is performing at an all-time low. Therefore, the mutual funds are also performing poorly, since a lot of the mutual funds are invested in the stock market.

This is a big problem for a lot of people who have put their life savings and trust into the hands of banks, hoping to have enough money available for their retirement.

The other problem is that most of these investment advisors are not very experienced and are only following the direction they were given in their limited training.

Let's look at an example:

Let's say you've just turned 60. You have worked hard all your life and you have even saved a sizable nest egg. However, you cannot retire because if you just live off your nest egg, it will run out pretty fast.

You may run out of money before you run out of life.

You may have tried to find good investments but unfortunately, those are hard to come by. Your latest research showed that you could get 2% on a Guaranteed Investment Certificate (GIC). That's crazy!!

You decided to pull all your money out of the stock market because you were afraid that another major drop would destroy your savings and you would never be able to retire.

> ***How are you ever going to retire when there is no place left to safely invest your money?***

And pretty soon, you will be forced to retire.

Unfortunately, not being able to retire is the story for many people who don't have a company or government pension plan.

For example, let's say you have a savings of $1,000,000. I think most people would agree that this is a good size nest egg.

Nonetheless, if you invest that $1M at only 2%, that means you would only be getting $20,000 per year. Now I know you have all heard that you don't need as much money when you retire because you don't have as many expenses, but $20,000 is ridiculous, especially with inflation.

You probably have your house paid off. You no longer have kids to support because they are grown up and left the house.

> ***I don't know about you, but I didn't work all my life to try and get by on $20,000 a year.***

Many people are continuing to work well past their retirement age, earning their high salary, because they haven't figured out any alternatives. But what happens when they are forced to retire?

I have a friend who is 60 years old and he makes about $250K a year. He has a net worth of over $1M. Despite the great income, he can't retire. He says he can retire and live off his savings until the day those savings have run out. Assuming he reduces his income from $250K to $100K a year and starts withdrawing from his nest egg. That means he only has about 10 years before his savings run out … and then what?

Desperate parents are finding themselves moving in with their children, which is what's happening to many aging people.

Let us assume, in our example above that my friend can live off $50K per year. That's still only 20 years until he has run out of money. But now he is still only 80 years old when his money runs out. Many people are living past 80 these days.

Think about it for a moment. Just how much would $50K be able to buy in 20 years' time, with inflation the way it is? Just this last year saw an inflation rate of 1.5%.

The retirement situation is bleak for a lot of people in Canada and the United States. The system people have trusted, and they were relying on, is broke.

This retirement issue is a major problem for a lot of Canadians and Americans.

So, what is the solution to the investment retirement problem?

3.2 - Time to Take Back Control of Your Finances

So, why are there so many people not able to retire?

For too many years, people have been brainwashed about how they should be handling their investments. They were told to just work at their jobs and let the experts handle their investments. They were told to just work at their 9 to 5 jobs and not to worry about their finances. All they had to do was just pay their bills, put aside some play money and then take the rest of their money and invest it with an expert.

So, what went wrong?

People gave up control of their investments!

Most people I talk to today have no idea where their money is invested or even how their investments are performing. Basically, they have no control over their investments. I asked someone the other day where they had their money invested. They said all their money was invested in an RRSP. I told them an RRSP is an account, not an investment. They didn't understand.

Most people have no idea what stock or company that they have their money invested in and how well that stock has been performing; or how poorly that stock has been performing. And it would be very difficult to track since most people are invested in mutual funds, which is a fund that invests in many stocks and/or bonds. Even the mutual fund managers can't do a good job because the stock market is so volatile. That's another reason we have the problem that we have today.

One problem with the lack of financial control is that, no matter what you do, you can't change the outcome of your investment because your investment represents a minor share in a large corporation. You can't call the CEO of Google and ask them to make a change in their search algorithm or call General Motors and tell them not to put a new type of brakes on that model of car.

The biggest problem I see with the stock market is the outside influencers.

An outside influencer, for example, can be some world event that happened and that could have had a negative effect on the price of a stock. And it's not that the performance of the company has been affected. It's the "anticipation" of what might happen to the company, as a result of this world event, that affects the price of the stock.

For example, recent US election results almost caused the stock market to crash during the day of the election, which resulted in wall street halting trading for that day. And it was all because of the uncertainty of what may or may not happen. It had nothing to do with the performance of any of these companies. And that's just the US markets.

So, what can people do to protect their savings? About the only thing they can do is pull their money out of that investment.

For many years, people have been told to invest their hard-earned money into mutual funds and a good fund manager will help them direct their money into a fund that makes sense for them. There are many types of mutual funds available and people are directed to invest in different funds, depending on the characteristics of the person and the special mix of the fund.

Mutual fund advisors direct people's investments based on many factors such as risk tolerance, age, business sector, etc. They could also direct those people's investments into several different mutual funds and not just one. This is what the mutual fund advisors call *diversification*.

Investment advisors diversify people's investments by investing their money into many different companies that are in different sectors and that have different investment strategies (growth or income). But it's all still just one asset class. Stocks and maybe bonds. I don't think this is diversification.

Diversifying your investment portfolio is not done by investing in different stocks. It's done by investing in different asset classes.

Different asset classes are stocks, bonds, gold, silver, and especially real estate.

Real estate investing, if done properly, can give you much better control over your investments.

The other big problem with mutual funds is that some of them charge a high management fee to have your money invested with them. I'm not going to go into any more detail about how mutual funds work because I am basically saying that mutual funds aren't working for you anymore, so get out. And here's another crazy thing.

Most people giving financial recommendations on which stock or mutual fund to choose, have less money invested (or no money invested) than the person they are making the recommendations to.

They probably have less money in their own savings, than their clients do. So how can they be giving financial advice to someone else?

The other situation is that some people think they can manage their own investment portfolio so, instead of investing in a mutual fund, they go to a stockbroker and buy the latest hottest stock. They heard about this stock from their hairdresser's second cousin, so it must be good.

It is my experience that the people who are successful in the stock market, whether it's through mutual funds or through stocks, are successful because they have a well thought out strategy with a very experienced broker and they have enough money to make it interesting for that broker.

Investing in the stock market is gambling ... pure and simple. If you win, sometimes you win big. But if you lose ... it really hurts.

So why do people invest in mutual funds? Because they are told it is safe. And mutual funds had been doing well for many years. But times have changed. The stock market has become highly volatile. About the only guaranteed investments are GICs or Savings accounts.

I had someone come up to me the other day and say *"Jim... I have $200,000. If I just gave it to you what kind of return can you give me."* He had just pulled all of his money out of the stock market and was about to put it into a GIC at 2%, which he thought was ridiculous,

People are lost now. They have no idea what to do. People don't know where to invest their money and how to plan for retirement. And the government isn't helping them either.

The government continues to offer people Registered Investment accounts (RRSPs, etc.) for the same type of investments … stocks, bonds, and mutual funds. Sure, maybe you thought you were safer with your bank advisor or another financial planner, but if your money is invested at rates that are lower than the cost of living, you are actually losing money,

But it's OK … the big banks are looking out for you, right?

And if you lose money, you can always blame the banks.

Fortunately, there are much better alternatives that provide higher rates of return, lower risk, and that are fully secured. And it puts you, the investor, back in control of your investments, and with only a little bit of planning and oversight.

Now that's passive investing done the right way.

3.3 - Are Your Savings Losing Value?

Where are people supposed to invest their savings? Where can they invest their money safely? Where can their money be secure?

There aren't many safe places left to invest your money ... if any.

Contrary to popular thinking, there has never really been a secure place to invest your money that pays a decent return. The only real safe investment is a Guaranteed Investment Certificate (GIC), and lately, that type of investment has NOT been providing a very good return. There was a time when you could get Canada Savings Bonds (CSB) that earned double-digit returns. In 1981 a CSB was paying 19.5%. In 2017, a CSB was paying only 1.4%. Those days of earning high returns on a secured investment are long gone.

In addition, what about the people who are looking to save for their retirement but they are not there yet. They are hoping to put their money is some type of registered account (RRSP or TFSA) and invest it in a high yield investment. Well, if that investment is a GIC, and it's only paying 1.4%, there's not a lot of wealth accumulation happening. With that type of return, people are barely keeping ahead of inflation. Moreover, if the investment is being made outside of a registered tax account, there are income taxes that have to be paid.

For example, let's say John is able to put aside $500 a month in his RRSP and that money is invested into a GIC earning an interest of only 2% per year. After a year, each monthly contribution of $500 is only worth $510. Even with compound interest, it's going to take a long time to create wealth while earning only 2%, even if the tax is deferred. The tax is deferred because the interest is being earned inside a registered tax account. And if you are investing in a GIC outside of a registered tax account the situation is even worse.

John continues to work hard, saves that $500 a month and cuts back on a lot of pleasures so he can reach his savings target, only to find out he can't retire because of the reasons we have just mentioned. His money is barely increasing in value because of the cost of living and inflation.

> ***It's important to make sure that you SAVE smart and INVEST smart.***

If you don't save smart and invest smart, all your hard work was for nothing. There are lots of people working long hours, working at 2 jobs, just so they can earn enough to make a living. So, when people invest their money, they should make sure they are investing it wisely.

For the longest time, people have been told that mutual funds are safe, or at least that was the perception for a lot of people. THIS IS NOT TRUE.

> ***There are better ways to invest your money than investing in mutual funds, stocks, and bonds.***

For example, there are a lot of ways that you can invest in Real Estate that are much safer and secure if done properly. You have to take control of your investments and make sure that you are investing wisely. Wise investing does not just mean being so risk-averse that your earnings are actually losing money. This is what happens when you don't take the time to do your research and properly analyze the different investment opportunities. It's time to take back control of your investments from the big financial institutions.

Now I'm not saying you can't make good returns in the stock market. But most people don't want to take the time to invest in the stock market properly. You have to have a good plan with a good broker and you need time. You need time to analyze and understand the companies that you are thinking about investing in. Yes, your stockbroker needs to analyze these companies for you and make recommendations for you, but you also need to be able to understand why these companies are a good investment for you.

And even if you do all that analysis, you still don't have control over your investments because you have no influence on the company you are investing in. You can't respond to any sudden changes in the market or changes in the economy that could grossly affect that company and your investment.

And what about inflation? Inflation could actually eat up your earnings. Below is a table of the annual inflation rate in Canada at the end of December each year. The data is for each of the past 10 years. I have also shown the net impact of a 2% investment return adjusted for that inflation.

Year	Inflation	Net Return if 2%	Cumulative Net
2015	1.61%	2.0-1.61 = 0.39%	0.39%
2014	1.47%	2.0-1.47 = 0.53%	0.92%
2013	1.24%	2.0-1.24 = 0.76%	1.68%
2012	0.83%	2.0-0.83 = 1.17%	2.85%
2011	2.30%	2.0-2.30 =**-0.30%**	2.55%
2010	2.35%	2.0-2.35 =**-0.35%**	2.20%
2009	1.32%	2.0-1.32 = 0.68%	2.88%
2008	1.16%	2.0-1.16 = 0.84%	3.72%
2007	2.38%	2.0-2.38 =**-0.38%**	3.34%
2006	1.67%	2.0-1.67 = 0.33%	3.67%

So, the future value of the $500 in 10 years, adjusted for inflation, is 3.67% x $500 = a $18.35 increase. That's not a lot to show for a 10-year return and for all the hard work it took you to earn that $500 in the first place. There were actually 3 years where the investment didn't make enough just to keep up with inflation.

You always have to think of the future value of the dollar when looking at your investments, especially with such a low rate of return. Future value takes inflation into account.

> ***An investment strategy based strictly on the preservation of capital does not provide any wealth accumulation at all.***

As you can see, that $500 has really only increased by $18.35. Even though the actual dollar value of the investment has risen to about $609.50, the buying power of that investment is only worth $518.75 in today's dollars. This is not something people tend to think about when they look at the net value of their investment. People just look at the dollar value of their investment and think it has risen by over $100, as is the case in this example.

This type of investment strategy is the equivalent of putting your money under your mattress and forgetting about it. I'm not sure which is more irresponsible … not investing your money or investing it into such a low yield investment that just barely beats inflation.

There's another old saying. *"There is no difference between someone who can read and doesn't and someone who cannot read."*. A variation of this saying can be applied to investing as follows.

> ***"There's no difference between someone who invests in the wrong thing and someone who doesn't invest at all."***

People are so afraid of losing their money because of the high volatility and poor performance they have seen in the stock market lately. Now there are certainly other considerations depending on your age and your accumulated savings to date. For example, the older you are and the smaller the amount of savings you have … the more risk-averse you need to be.

But there's a much easier way to make money outside of the stock market and it's very passive. However, you have to do your own due diligence. There are several ways to invest safely in real estate and yield much higher returns.

IF YOU WOULD LIKE MORE INFORMATION ON OUR PROGRAMS AND HOW WE MIGHT BE ABLE TO HELP, CHECK OUT THIS WEBSITE: **WWW.INVESTNOWINC.COM**

CHAPTER 4

Traditional Investing

In this chapter, you will learn how traditional investing works and how traditional investing may not be the right solution for you. For many years people have been told to seek out an investment advisor for their investment needs. A certified investment advisor will review a person's financial situation and, based on their situation, would then lay out an investment plan for this person's future. The investment advisor seemed quite capable. After all, he had lots of certifications so he must have known what he was doing.

As a result of blindly following these investment advisors, people are finding themselves in dire straits. Most people don't have enough money to retire. Or, the more fortunate ones have some money, but they can't find the right investments to invest in. For example, the investments that their investment advisor is suggesting that they invest in may only be paying them 2%. Even if you have saved $1,000,000, a 2% annual return on a $1,000,000 investment portfolio is only $20,000 a year. That's pretty much minimum wage. As a result, people are looking for a better investment that would pay them, say, a 10% annual return. A 10% return is not that hard to find in real estate if you know where to look and who to talk to.

The other problem today is that the investment advisor is not able to help them find real estate investments because they are only licensed to sell securities. The only way their investment advisor can diversify their investment portfolio is by diversifying across multiple stocks or mutual funds.

The investment advisor tells their client that they need to invest in a balanced fund or an equity fund or an income fund. And when their portfolio has lost significant value because their investments are down, they tell them to *"hold on ... the market is going to come back"*.

Or worse, the investment advisor suggests to their clients that they buy more of the same stock because the stock is worth less so they can buy a lot more of the same stock at a much lower price. It's like the stock is on sale. They even have a name for this strategy. It's called "dollar-cost averaging". But of course, this only works if the failing stock does increase in value again.

People are left to their own devices and are forced to go out and learn about real estate investing or some other alternative investment strategy.

There are a lot of people who are working well past their desired retirement age because they did not take care of their own financial planning and they have left it up to their investment advisor. It's important to take control of your own investment planning and your overall financial situation.

4.1 - Traditional Investing

For years, Canadians have relied on other people to help them with their investments and to help them with their long-term savings and retirement planning. These "other" people, such as investment advisors, have been directing people to invest in traditional investments, such as stocks and bonds.

Discovery

The following is how traditional investing usually works.

People would book an appointment with their investment advisor and they would sit down with them and go over their own investment criteria. There are a number of questions an investment advisor would ask their clients to see what type of investments might be right for them.

Some questions an investment advisor might ask a potential investor are:

- How much money do they have to invest with and how much money can they contribute on a monthly basis?
- What are their long-term income goals?
- How old are they and at what age do they plan on retiring?
- What is their risk tolerance?
- What other investments do they have?

Using this information, an investment advisor would plug it into their magical program that would spew out recommendations for the individual or couple.

The problem with this type of financial planning is that there is no certainty (there never really is with any investment) and there are too many variables that would impact the investment plan. There is no possible way to determine the performance of any investment that is based strictly on stocks and bonds.

And what if there was a change in the investor's employment or their income? How would that affect their long-term plan?

Investments

Based on the information that was provided to them, these investment advisors would then make recommendations as to what the client should invest in. For the most part, these recommendations are focused on investing in the stock market in some form or another.

Stockbrokers are the most common type of investment advisor, but banks started getting into the game and started calling their people investment advisors as well. These investment advisors would, for the most part, recommend investing part of their client's portfolio into mutual funds, Guaranteed Investment Certificates (GICs) and even savings.

Mutual Funds

Mutual funds are the stock market's way of implying diversification by investing in multiple companies in various ways. A mutual fund can be diversified in many ways.

1. Invest in multiple mutual funds
2. Invest in Canadian and US stocks within a fund
3. Invest in equity growth stocks and income-earning stocks within a fund
4. Invest in different sectors (e.g. financial, oil, manufacturing, technology, etc.) within one mutual fund
5. Invest in stocks and bonds within a fund

Diversification in a mutual fund is very deceiving. For the most part, all the investments are still stocks and bonds.

In my opinion, diversification really only occurs when your money is invested in several different asset classes. Stocks, bonds, gold and, of course, real estate.

Guaranteed Investment Certificates (GICs)

GICs are mostly available from banks and insurance companies. GICs earn a nominal rate of interest and are usually locked in for a period of time, which means you can't withdraw your money without a penalty. The rates are guaranteed during your GIC term. The longer the term, usually the higher the rate of return. At the time of this writing, the highest rate of interest was 2.5% for a 5-year term GIC.

A GIC is you lending your money to the bank so they can loan it back to you or someone else at a much higher rate. These bank loans are usually personal loans or mortgage loans. Because the funds are locked in, the banks can invest that money for the long term as well. Check out Rate Hub for the current GIC rates in Canada: https://www.ratehub.ca/gics/best-gic-rates

If you lend your money to the bank at a rate of 2.5%, in the form of a GIC, and then the bank loans it out as a personal loan at a rate of 7%, they make 4.5% on your money. Not a bad margin.

Savings Accounts

Savings accounts are similar to GICs, except the rates are not guaranteed and are subject to change at any time. Savings accounts typically earn a lot less than a GIC because savings accounts are open and more liquid. That means that you can withdraw your money at any time. Check out Rate Hub for current Savings Account rates in Canada: https://www.ratehub.ca/savings-accounts/best-savings-accounts

Discount Brokerages and Online Trading

To make matters even worse people started using online trading platforms and discount brokerages. They have lost confidence in their investment advisor so they think they can do their own trading with no advice from their brokers. Plus, they take pride in doing their own trades.

I can remember a lot of people bragging about the money they made on their investments. For example, 1 person I was talking to had just made a 20% return on one of their investments. It turns out that they only had about 1/10 of their portfolio invested. The balance of their portfolio was sitting in a savings account. So, their 20% return on that portion represented about a 2% return for their entire portfolio.

Day Trading

Day trading is a whole different ball game altogether. And I really mean game. This is where people buy stocks hoping that they are going to benefit from a change in price in a very short period, usually 1 day. For example, they buy a stock in the morning for $10 and sell it at the end of the day for $11 and they make $1 on the trade. That's a 10% return on their investment in only 1 day. So, if you have invested $100,000, you would have made $10,000. Not bad for 1 days' worth of work. However, not all of these investments make a 10% return, and many of the investments actually lose money.

The idea is that they will buy enough different stocks and hope that more stocks go up in value than the ones that go down in value. People I know who have tried this strategy spend a lot of time doing it. This can become a full-time job and a full-time obsession.

RRSPs (tax account)

Some people actually think their RRSP is an investment. You ask some people what type of investments they have and they tell you they have an RRSP.

> ***An RRSP, or another type of registered account, is simply a vehicle that helps you defer your income tax and shelter your income earned inside your RRSP from income tax.***

Funds inside your RRSP can be invested in several types of investments. Some of these types of investments include GICs, stocks, bonds, mutual funds, and mortgages.

In real estate investing, mortgages are a very popular type of passive investing. People can invest in mortgages, within their RRSP, as long as the mortgage is not on a property that they own themselves. This is called arms-length mortgage investing.

The mortgage must be administered by a third-party trustee. Because you are responsible for identifying the mortgage investment opportunity, this type of investment is referred to as a self-directed RRSP and needs a special account set up and managed by a trustee.

For a full list of eligible investments that can be made inside your registered account in Canada, check out:
http://www.cra-arc.gc.ca/tx/tchncl/ncmtx/fls/s3/f10/s3-f10-c1-eng.html

Traditional investments are becoming less reliable and people are starting to look for alternatives, such as self-directed mortgage investing and real estate investing.

4.2 - Investment Advisors

One of the challenges investors are faced with when looking to invest in the stock market is finding a good investment advisor.

There are many people who call themselves investment advisors. Moreover, there are many certifications and designations available for investment advisors. In addition, there are also a few governing bodies that oversee all these investment advisors. Confused yet?

Investment Advisors (IAs) work for investment dealers that trade in securities. The largest firms in Canada are owned by banks, but there are also a number of independent ones. The investment advisor must be registered with the securities regulators to be able to provide investment advice and to be able to buy and sell investment products such as stocks, bonds, and mutual funds.

In Canada, investment advisors must be licensed under one of two organizations. The first is the Investment Industry Regulatory Organization of Canada (IIROC). Advisers licensed through the IIROC can deal in Mutual Funds, individual stocks and exchange-traded funds (ETFs). The Mutual Funds Dealers Association (MFDA) is the other association people are licensed through. The MFDA can only deal with mutual funds.

There are other investment advisors out there that are licensed to sell insurance and that can also sell other types of investments other than mutual funds, stocks, and ETFs.

Then, there are the designated *'Financial Planners'* who are another type of investment advisor and who are not licensed to sell any of the above products just mentioned. They are only licensed to give investment advice.

Before selecting an Investment Advisor, you can always check to see if they are actually registered.

The Canadian Securities Administrators is an umbrella organization that oversees the regulations for the 10 provincial securities regulators in Canada. You can search their database for any investment advisor at *www.aretheyregistered.ca*. Anyone licensed by the MFDA or the IIROC, or who holds the portfolio manager designation, should appear in this database. Insurance and financial planners will not appear in the database unless they are also a licensed investment advisor. Another website, the CSA website (*www.securities-administrators.ca*) allows you to see if your licensed advisor has ever gotten into trouble.

Know Your Client and Suitability

Most advisors in Canada are held to what is called the "suitability standard." This means that they must be able to demonstrate that an investment is appropriate for an individual investor. In other words, is the investment right for the client, based on the client's goals, experience, income, and risk tolerance? Most investment advisors have a form that they fill out with their clients. This helps the advisor to get to know their client better by asking them questions related to such things as age, retirement goals, risk tolerance, and investment goals.

For example, following this suitability standard, an investment advisor should not be recommending that a person invest 100% of their investment portfolio into high-risk stocks if that is the only source of income for that person and if that person is 70 years old. That type of investment for that person would be deemed unsuitable. A more conservative investment would be more appropriate for someone meeting that profile. The investment should be more conservative in nature for that person.

Training

The Canadian Securities Institute offers courses and certifications so people can sell securities such as stocks and bonds, mutual funds, options, and derivatives, but not private investments and insurance. There are also several courses on how to *manage* an investment portfolio for their clients.

Here's a list of all the Certifications that are available through the CSI for each of the business lines. While these certifications may provide additional information for the certification holder, it is very confusing for the clients as to what each of these certifications actually means and how these certifications can benefit the client:

BUSINESS BANKING

Certificate in Commercial Credit
Certificate in Small Business Banking

FINANCIAL PLANNING

Certificate in Advanced Mutual Funds Advice
Certificate in Financial Services Advice
Certificate in Personal Banking
Personal Financial Planner (PFP®) designation

INVESTMENT MANAGEMENT & TRADING

Certificate in Advanced Investment Advice
Certificate in Advanced Mutual Funds Advice
Certificate in Derivatives Market Strategies
Certificate in Equity Trading and Sales
Certificate in Fixed Income Trading and Sales
Certificate in Investment Dealer Compliance
Chartered Investment Manager (CIM®) designation
Fellow of CSI (FCSI®)

LEADERSHIP, MANAGEMENT & COMPLIANCE

CERTIFICATE IN BANKING MANAGEMENT
CERTIFICATE IN INVESTMENT DEALER COMPLIANCE
FELLOW OF CSI (FCSI®)

RETAIL BANKING

CERTIFICATE IN BANKING MANAGEMENT
CERTIFICATE IN FINANCIAL SERVICES ADVICE
CERTIFICATE IN PERSONAL BANKING
PERSONAL FINANCIAL PLANNER (PFP®) DESIGNATION

WEALTH MANAGEMENT

CERTIFICATE IN ADVANCED INVESTMENT ADVICE
CERTIFICATE IN ESTATE PLANNING AND TRUST STRATEGY
CERTIFICATE IN RETIREMENT STRATEGY
CERTIFIED INTERNATIONAL WEALTH MANAGER (CIWM) DESIGNATION
MTI – ESTATE AND TRUST PROFESSIONAL

The main course required to allow an individual to deal with stocks is CSI's *Canadian Securities Course.*

There are several other firms that offer investment education. A few of them are the *IFSE Institute*, *Institute of Canadian Bankers*, *CFA Institute*, *Advocis*, and the *RESP Dealers Association of Canada.*

Candidates interested in selling life insurance products in Canada, including annuities, must complete the *Life License Qualification Program (LLQP)* (except in Quebec, where life insurance licensing is handled by the *Autorité des Marchés Financiers*).

CFP – Certified Financial Planner

This seems to be the most sought-after certification for financial planners. To achieve this certification, you must take the course approved by the *Financial Planning Standards Council*. Then, you must write and pass the exam. Afterward, you need three years of direct financial planning experience.

I would suggest that if you want to hire a financial advisor, the CFP is the main designation that you want to look for. It really covers all the subject areas necessary for financial planning.

CFA – Chartered Financial Analyst

The CFA designation is more appropriate for investment management, rather than financial planning. Portfolio managers and investment analysts are the key jobs for this designation. It is, however, common for CFA graduates to become financial planners. This is probably the hardest designation to get. You have to write three lengthy exams and you need to have four years of related investment experience.

IFIC – Investment Funds in Canada

This course is the easiest financial planning course available. It is the minimum qualification to sell mutual funds in Canada. How easy is it? Some people I know actually wrote the exam without studying and passed easily.

The IFIC is suitable for a beginning investor, however, I'm not sure if it's worth the money, given the number of financial advice articles that are available on the web. The IFIC covers basic financial planning and mutual funds. If your (future) job involves selling mutual funds or giving advice on mutual funds, then you will need to take this course.

CSC (Canadian Securities Course)

This course is a much harder course than the IFIC course. The material is more detailed and there is a lot more material that you will have to cover. Not only does this course cover all the same material from the IFIC it also covers topics like stocks, options, and bonds.

For any job involving investments, other than mutual funds, the CSC is usually mandatory. A broker's assistant would need this and call center employees for discount brokerages should take this.

For investment advisors, this is a decent course to take. It's a fair bit of work, but you will learn quite a bit.

This course is self-study with a written exam. It is suggested that 135-200 hours of study are necessary and to properly prepare for and pass the exam. Today, there are roughly 18,000 active CFPs in Canada, which makes it the most popular financial-advice designation.

4.3 - Traditional Diversification

One way to reduce the risk of your investments is by diversifying. However, you must know how to diversify properly.

Ask any investment advisor or financial planner and they will tell you that the number one way to reduce your risk is to diversify your portfolio by investing in different stocks or mutual funds in different sectors.

But I have heard some people say that the best way to reduce your risk is to invest in only one thing and to become very knowledgeable about that one thing. For me, real estate is the number one thing.

"The way to become rich is to put all your eggs in one basket and then watch that basket"

— Andrew Carnegie

"Diversification is protection against ignorance. It makes little sense [to diversify] if you know what you are doing"

— Warren Buffet

However, most people don't know what they are doing. They have taken little or no time to learn about their investments. They have lost control and have given control to their financial advisors.

The other big problem with diversification is that, if you mitigate risk by using one sector's gains to offset another sector's losses, you would end up reducing your overall returns. The reverse is also true. One sector's losses can be offset by another sector's gains, achieving the same overall averaging effect.

For example, you may be making a return of 10% in an investment that is in the oil and gas sector and but only making a return of 2% on another investment in the financial sector. The financial sector investment, in this example, has effectively pulled down the oil and gas sector investment. Therefore, your average return is now only 6% overall. Still a pretty good return in today's markets.

A better strategy would be to become an expert in either one of those sectors and invest more wisely in the individual stocks within that sector. Or you can always look at alternative investments such as real estate.

> ***Diversification is also very difficult for smaller portfolios since there isn't much money to spread around to many different investments.***

To diversify your investment means to spread your investment money across several different investments. To most investment advisors, this means putting your money into different stocks and/or different mutual funds. The problem with that type of diversification is that it's still in the same asset class. ALL your money is still invested in stocks and bonds. Real estate brings into play another level of diversification by adding a whole different asset class.

The reason why people want to diversify is so that they are not "putting all of their eggs in one basket". They want to reduce their exposure to a specific investment. A "stock only" diversification strategy could mean investing in stocks but across different sectors. For example, some stocks can be held in oil and gas companies while other stocks can be simultaneously held in financial companies with the remaining stocks held in technology companies. Your portfolio appears to be 'diversified' — but it's ALL just stocks!

When some people are looking to invest in stocks, they focus on investing in a specific sector because they think that the sector will help them reach their financial goals. For example, some sectors may be less volatile, which would appeal to investors who are focused on predictability and capital preservation.

Meanwhile, other sectors that have more growth potential and higher volatility may appeal to investors with higher risk tolerance.

Here are some ways people diversify within the stock market:

Invest in Many Companies

One way a person may diversify their stock investments is by investing in several different stocks. These stocks may all be in the same sector or spread across several different sectors. There was no real analysis done to determine which sector to invest in. They just like the stock. For example, someone may have investments in Google and Walmart, just because they like the performance of these companies.

This type of investment is good as long as the investor monitors these companies and understands what these companies are going to do in the long term. A good investment advisor can help the investor with the analysis of the company. This is what a good advisor should be doing for them. The problem with this strategy is that the investor can't really be an expert on too many companies — even with the help of a good advisor. This model is actually similar to non-diversification and is fairly close to what Andrew Carnegie and Warren Buffet were suggesting in their statements above.

Another variation of investing in different stocks is to invest in different mutual funds. Again, there was no actual evaluation done for the performance of the sector, or the fund, for that matter. The investor just decided they liked a particular fund and invested in it.

Invest in Many Sectors

One of the most common ways investors are told to diversify their portfolio is to invest in different sectors. You can do this by investing in individual stocks in different sectors or by investing in mutual funds in different sectors. Some mutual funds will make diversifying easier for you by having the fund invest in different sectors.

The global industry classification system divides the economy into 10 sectors:

ENERGY - OIL AND GAS PRODUCTION
FINANCIALS - INVESTMENT BANKS, INSURANCE
MATERIALS - MANUFACTURERS
INDUSTRIALS - MACHINERY PROVIDERS
UTILITIES - RETAIL ELECTRIC AND GAS PROVIDERS
INFORMATION TECHNOLOGY - SOFTWARE, HARDWARE PROVIDERS
TELECOMMUNICATION SERVICES - PHONE SERVICES, CABLE PROVIDERS
CONSUMER DISCRETIONARY - RETAIL SHOPPING
CONSUMER STAPLES - GROCERIES
HEALTHCARE - PHARMACEUTICAL, MEDICAL FACILITIES

The investor would typically look for stocks or mutual funds that they like and that meet their investment objectives, and then they invest in two or more sectors. Again, this is a lot of work for an individual investor to monitor and keep track of all their investments in several different sectors. Some mutual funds are already set-up where they diversify into two or more sectors — so you can choose the ones that make sense for you. For example, you could invest in a mutual fund, that has 50% of its investments in the financial sector and the other half in the technology sector.

Invest in Income and Equity Stocks

Another type of diversification, that is more of a financial planning objective, is to invest in income and equity growth stocks. Some stocks pay higher regular dividends which could provide an income base for investors. Other stocks may minimize their dividend payout and focus more on stock price growth, which is more of a long-term strategy.

Choosing a combination of short-term dividends stocks and long-term growth stocks may make sense from a financial planning perspective, rather than as a diversification strategy with the objective of reducing risk.

Diversification in real estate is simple and can be done in many ways. Very active full-time real estate investors may invest in assignments and flips for short term income and use rentals for long term growth. These full time, active real estate investors generally know what they are doing. This type of diversification is contained within the same asset class, otherwise known as "real estate". Furthermore, if you invest wisely, and you know what you are doing, you can control the outcome of most real estate projects.

Summary

To diversify in a stock-only strategy means to spread your investment money across several stocks and/or mutual funds. For the average investor, this strategy may not be the right solution. An alternative route of diversification is to look at investing in other asset classes, such as real estate.

CHAPTER 5

Real Estate Investing: The Alternative

People have been investing in traditional investments (stocks and bonds) for a long time. The nice thing about this type of investing is that it is very passive. You meet with your stockbroker or financial advisor and you discuss your portfolio and they make recommendations. Subsequently, with your permission, and their recommendations, they take your money and invest it.

The problem with this type of investing is that it is very passive and, because of that, most investors have never had to take responsibility for their investments. The other big problem with this approach is that the stock market is very volatile and provides inconsistent returns. Taking these problems into consideration, people have started looking at real estate as an alternative to the stock market.

The aggressive real estate investors learn a little bit about real estate investing, go out, and start buying some properties right away. The problem with this strategy is that they are buying properties without having a clear understanding of what their goals are and how their real estate investments can satisfy those goals.

Real estate investing can provide income-type returns and/or growth-type returns. It's also important to know what you are looking for. Are you looking for a steady income stream or can you wait for equity growth?

For example, if you can't decide what your goal is, you could end up investing in rentals, which is really a growth strategy. You were really looking for an investment that provides an income stream. Mortgage investing or fix and flips might be more appropriate for you if you are looking for short-term income.

There are several different real estate investment strategies, each of which come with their own challenges and their own income stream. Real estate investing can also have a lot of problems if you don't know what you are doing. Moreover, the majority of people go into real estate without knowing what they are doing. These real estate investors often lose money as a result. Compared to stock trading, real estate investing is not a very passive investment strategy.

Rentals require managing. Fix and flips also require management skills. The same thing applies to rent to own strategies. Wholesaling is like having a job because you are always looking for deals.

So, if you are looking for a passive alternative to the stock market, you should not own real estate. But you can still invest in real estate if you have the cash.

The best passive real estate investments are private mortgages and private equity deals. People don't realize that they can actually earn money by lending it to other people and having that loan secured by a property through a mortgage charge. Banks operate this way and you can too! However, you can actually charge more than the banks, since your prospective borrowers would often be people who can't get their financing from the bank.

Joint ventures are another way in which you can become a passive real estate investor. However, there's no continuity and you are always investing in new ventures with new partners with new risks and challenges. Joint ventures require a little bit more time than mortgage or equity investing.

5.1 Real Estate Investing

Real estate has been a favorite investment of people for many years. One of the famous quotes is

"invest in Real Estate, they aren't making any more of it".

There are probably just as many ways to invest in real estate as there are to invest in the stock market. The trick to real estate investing is to focus on the investment strategy that makes the most sense for you, that is aligned with your goals.

Now, I could write a whole book on the many ways to invest in real estate (and I have) but the purpose of *this* book is to focus on real estate investing as an alternative to the stock market, so I will focus on the more *passive* ways to make money in real estate. Also, these passive strategies are more closely related to how people invest in the stock market.

Now I'm sure that you have watched all the TV shows that show you how to make money investing in real estate. And you probably know a few people who have made money investing with real estate. And you might even know a few people who have lost some money investing in real estate, which is more common than you think. Therefore, the trick is to choose strategies that make you a good return, that are secured with low risk and that are fairly passive.

The biggest problem with real estate investing is that most people do it wrong.

Most people get into the wrong real estate investment strategy that isn't aligned with their goals. They invest in the wrong project because they don't know what they are doing. They go to a couple of free real estate seminars and read a couple of books and think they have it all figured out. One of the best things you can do as an active real estate investor is to get professional training and to hire a professional coach/mentor. You have to be willing to learn. I heard this saying once:

"You can't learn what you think you already know"

Just because you went to a couple of seminars and read a couple of books, that doesn't make you an expert. Buying a rental property and having to deal with bad tenants and major repairs is a great way to learn. Doing a fix and flip and losing $20K because you did a bunch of things wrong, is another great way to learn. Hiring someone to coach you and to work with you is a much cheaper and more positive way to learn. You learn from *your coach's* mistakes, so you don't have to suffer the same pain and financial loss that they already have. But this is only if you want to be an active real estate investor. This book is about becoming a passive real estate investor.

Another big mistake I made as a beginner real estate investor was thinking I could do it all myself. I did this mostly because I was trying to save money.

When I was just starting out as a real estate investor I wrote my own offers, rather than using a realtor. I did this for my private deals. I actually used contracts that I got from one of the courses I took, and I didn't even get a lawyer involved until it was time to close.

When I first started, I was even doing my own property management. The thinking was that I would manage my own properties and then I could take on other people's properties and manage their properties. Being a property manager is not real estate investing ... it's a job. So, I had to hire someone to be a full-time property manager for me. And there isn't much money in property management. I ended up not doing much property management for other people since I had over 60 properties of my own. Oh, and I was doing all this while holding down a full-time consulting job.

Other problems beginner real estate investors make is that they don't get enough education. They invest too soon without understanding what they are doing. They don't do enough due diligence. They get impatient and don't take enough time to do a proper analysis.

I remember the first lease option investment I ever made. I was trying to implement the sandwich lease option strategy whereby I find a motivated seller to give up their property into our rent to own program. I was talking to many owners but no one seemed to be interested. The key here was to find a motivated seller who couldn't sell their property. Well after many months of approaching sellers, I ended up signing a deal with a seller that had a modular home that they couldn't sell. This ended up being the worst rent to own deal I ever did. The problem was that I had taken over their payments right away before I had found a tenant buyer for the rent to own program. The property remained empty for several months and I had to carry the house until we found a tenant buyer.

The other problem with this investment is that the house was not very attractive and I went through several tenant buyers before I finally gave the house back to the owner and never completed the deal with them. I learned a lot from that deal.

People think real estate investing is easier than it actually is.

The following are some of the ways to get involved with real estate and the risk, the return and the management involved with each. This is purely subjective and is based on my many years of investment experience.

Type	Risk	Return	Management
1. Wholesaling	Low	Low	Low
2. Fix and Flips	High	Med	High
3. Development	High	High	High

4. Rentals	Med	Med	High
5. Rent to Own	Med	Med	Low
6. Mortgages	Low	Med	Low

Most people who get into real estate investing do so because they think they can make lots of money. Some people are looking at real estate as an investment and some are looking at is as a career change. As a result, they get into the more "active" types of investing which are the majority of the investment strategies.

The successful real estate investors are the ones that end up making a career out of it.

A lot of times the returns in real estate investing aren't what the investors expect them to be and sometimes they end up losing a lot of money. Sure, it may look good on paper, but if you actually calculate the amount of time versus the return, you end up working for minimum wage and you don't even realize it.

At the start of an investment, everything looks good. Here's what you are going to make if the renovation goes as planned. Here's what you are going to make if you have perfect tenants who pay on time and never damage the property. Most people don't build in enough contingencies and ignore some real expenses.

For example, when people are analyzing rental properties, I see them leave out maintenance and property management expenses. They claim they will be managing the property and doing the repairs themselves. So, I ask them if they work for free. In addition, with an approach like that, it's hard to scale the business. I tried to do it myself for a while but ended up hiring a full-time property manager on location, a full-time property manager in my head office and a maintenance crew. The result was that the properties no longer had a positive cash flow because of all these extra costs.

But rental properties are not meant to be an income investment. They are more of a buy and hold long-term strategy that will pay off after about 10 years, once the mortgage is paid down considerably and once the value of the property has increased. Don't ever make the mistake of thinking rentals produce a monthly income. One bad tenant or one bad repair could wipe out your monthly cash flow for months, even years.

So, the best way for busy people to invest in real estate is for them to invest in more passive real estate investments, such as mortgage investments and private equity investments.

5.2 - Different Types of Real Estate Investing

There are many different real estate investment strategies. Each comes with its own advantages and disadvantages. Here's a brief overview of some.

Buy, Rent and Hold (Rentals)

Rentals are probably the most common real estate investment strategy that most people know about. Rentals can be highly lucrative, and somewhat passive if done properly. It may take a bit of time to get educated on how and where to invest in rentals. You want to make sure that the property will cash flow positively and that the costs associated with maintenance and repairs are minimal. You must also bear the responsibility of making sure that the property is properly maintained. I know this sounds like a lot of work — and it can be if you don't have a good property manager in place.

The property has to take into account the cost of a property manager and the cost of the maintenance. Oh, and don't forget the vacancy allowance. All these costs combined can account for as much as 15% of your gross income and will considerably affect your overall cash flow.

When doing the financial analysis of a rental property, most real estate investors don't take into account all the expenses that are part of owning and renting out the property. They simply buy a property, usually a single-family home, and rent it out, hoping to make an income from the property. Getting a positive cash flow from a single-family rental property hardly ever happens and is the biggest misunderstanding in real estate investing.

In my opinion, the only way you can really make money with rentals is if you own a property with many units and the property is run by a property manager. This means owning a building with 20 or more units, for example. Now, this will vary by city and area. Furthermore, these types of investments usually require a significant down payment so most people can't invest in these types of properties.

For example, let's say you are looking to purchase a 20-unit apartment building for $2.5M. You would probably need about 25% as a down payment and another 5% for closing costs. Your total investment required would be $750K. For many new investors, an investment of this size is not possible. Furthermore, this may be their only investment so it would be a very risky investment.

Fix and Flips

The next most popular investment strategy is fix and flip investments. This strategy has been made popular over the years by all the TV shows about fixing and flipping a property.

This strategy can be very risky if you don't know what you are doing. I wouldn't recommend doing your first fix and flip by yourself. You may want to team up with someone who has already done a few of these — and has been very successful at it.

The biggest challenge with fix and flips are the unknowns. People buy a property for a price they think is the right price. Then, they estimate the costs required for the renovation. Next, they estimate the price at which they are going to sell the property at and finally, they estimate the time it will take to sell the property. The problem with all of this is that the numbers are estimates and almost never turn out exactly the way you estimated. Most of the actual costs are much higher than the estimates.

New investors tend to underestimate these numbers because they are anxious to get a deal. They have been looking for the right property for a long time and they are getting anxious. The key to fix and flips is that it's a numbers game.

You look at 100 properties. You analyze about 10 of these properties. You make an offer on 5 of these properties and you end up buying one of them.

There's an old saying in real estate that *"you make money when you buy"*.

What this means is that you want to make sure you are able to purchase the property for the best price possible. This will help when it comes to selling the property at the end of the "fix".

Most new investors underestimate the costs of the renovation.

A good rule of thumb is to add between 25% and 50% of your renovation costs to your estimates to account for unexpected problems.

Of course, everyone thinks their property is worth more than it really is on the open market. If your fix and flip project has an after-repair value (ARV) of $500K, be prepared to take less than what the fair market value is for similar properties. This will ensure a speedy sale and will reduce your carrying costs. One way to reduce your carrying costs is to pay all cash for your properties so you aren't burdened with high mortgage payments if the property doesn't sell fast.

Rent-to-Own

Another, not as popular a strategy is rent to own. This is really a variation of the buy, rent and hold strategy. The big difference between these 2 strategies is that instead of dealing with a tenant you are dealing with a tenant buyer. A tenant buyer is someone who will be renting the property with the expectation that they will be buying the property after a specified length of time.

A couple of advantages with the rent-to-own strategy are:

1. Maintenance - tenant buyers are usually made responsible for the ongoing maintenance and repairs of the property, whereas, in a standard rental agreement the landlord is responsible.

2. The other advantage of the rent to own strategy is that the cash flow is much greater in the initial stages of the agreement. The tenant buyer is usually asked to pay an upfront *'option consideration'* for the right to purchase the property within a specified timeframe, usually 3 to 5 years. Plus, the monthly rent payments are usually much higher in a rent to own deal because they include an amount that covers all the owner's costs as well as an amount that will be used as a rent credit that will go towards the down payment.

A couple of disadvantages with the rent to own strategy are:

1. Changing rules - The banks and mortgage are constantly changing their rules which may make it harder to qualify the tenant buyer under a rent to own application.

2. Credit Problems - The nature of a rent to own strategy is that you are dealing with people who couldn't get qualified through traditional lenders and traditional qualifications. They may be a higher risk than a regular tenant who has good credit.

Mortgage Lending

Another, not so well-known strategy, is mortgage lending. However, it is a very popular strategy within the inner circle of investors. This is where you lend homeowners or homebuyers money to be able to finance the purchase of a property. This is very common with investors buying houses, which is not necessarily a good thing since it increases the monthly expenses of having to service these additional financing costs. This increases the risk and reduces the cash flow for the investor.

In this strategy, you are basically acting as if you were the bank since you are the lender. You will lend money to the purchaser/owner. The interest rates of this loan are usually much higher than in traditional mortgages. The loan is secured on the title of the property by a mortgage. The loan can occupy any position: a first, second or even a third position. The lower the position (e.g. second as opposed to first), the higher the interest rate.

There are many variations of mortgage loans that I will cover in another section; examples of mortgages include traditional mortgages, private mortgages, and vendor take-back mortgages.

5.3 - Joint Ventures

Another way to invest in real estate with minimal involvement is through something called a joint venture.

A joint venture is simply when two or more parties come together for the benefit of a particular project. I have seen joint ventures where there are two parties and I have seen joint ventures where there are three or more parties. I am sure there are many deals out there with a lot more joint venture partners. For example, a sandwich lease option could be considered a type of joint venture with several parties involved.

In real estate investing, the purpose of a joint venture is to leverage the capabilities and skills of each of the parties involved to purchase a specific real estate investment. The joint venture could be for a buy-and-hold investment strategy, a fix and flip investment strategy or even a rent-to-own investment strategy. Some joint ventures can be incorporated as a separate business entity. This means that a company would be set up specifically for that project.

The advantage of having a corporation for the joint venture is that there is a limited liability and there are also some potential tax advantages. There will be some costs associated with setting up a corporation and managing the corporation but the costs may be well worth it.

Another reason you may want to set up a corporation is if you have multiple projects that you want to invest in while keeping the same parties involved. In this case, you'll have the ease of only having to set up the joint venture once and the rules will carry forward from project to project. In this case, you and your fellow partners would be in the position of being shareholders in the corporation. In other situations, you may want to set up a single corporation for each project. This all depends on the parties involved and your history of working with each other.

The most common joint venture is where an experienced real estate investor joins forces with another person who doesn't have the time or experience. This other person's contribution to the joint venture is usually some type of financing. This finance partner, or *money partner*, could provide the down payment and the renovation costs and even go and get a mortgage to finance the balance of the financing required for the property. The money partner is a very passive investor. that is until something goes wrong with the investment!

A typical joint venture structure I have seen for three people purchasing an investment property is as follows:

1. **Money Partner** - This partner will put up either all or most of the cash for the down payment, the closing costs and the renovation costs — if there are any. This is the passive investor role.

2. **Mortgage Partner** - The only involvement required of this partner is to get qualified for the mortgage and to have the mortgage issued in their name. This is also a very passive role.

3. **Real Estate Partner** - This is the person who does all the real estate related work such as locating the property, finding the tenants, doing the renovations, managing the deal, etc. This is an active investor.

I have seen joint ventures where one person puts up all the money and his partner did all the construction or renovation but failed to deliver on his part of the joint venture. The work was behind and they had run out of money. The money partner had to come in and invest more time and money to straighten things out. He had to fire his *real estate partner* and bring in another developer to finish the job.

His investment went from *passive* to very *active* when all these problems happened. The money partner had become responsible for managing all the work to make sure things didn't get out of hand again.

The key to a passive investment joint venture is to make sure you know what you're getting into. Make sure you know your development real estate partner. Confirm that your real estate partner has a proven track record of experience doing the kind of work that they are about to undertake.

Unfortunately, there is a dilemma that is quite common when joint ventures consist of family members. People will trust the other person because they are related to them which allows them to overlook necessarily qualities such as skills or experience in the field of real estate development and renovations.

It's also important to define the level of involvement of all the partners. In other words, what will each partner bring to the deal? In what ways will each person be involved?

The money partners are usually very passive. Regardless, sometimes these people want to be more involved than their active real estate partner would like them to be. For example, I had one money partner who wanted to approve the tenant buyers in a rent-to-own investment we were doing. I told him that if he wanted to be that type hands-on of person, then this venture wasn't right for him and he should look for other opportunities.

The other thing you need to be aware of when looking for a money partner is their financial viability and their level of financial commitment. I have had a couple of deals fall through because the money partner was not able to do what they said they would do. Either they didn't have the necessary funds to purchase the property and to do the renovations, or they weren't able to get approved for a mortgage.

To avoid unexpected problems with getting financing from the money partner, I usually ask them for a non-refundable upfront deposit. I also get them to get pre-approved for a mortgage beforehand. I get the deposit made out to my lawyer with written instructions that these funds are only to be used for activities related to the property identified in the joint venture.

> ***The goal of a real estate joint venture, just like any other real estate investment, is to make a profit.***

One of the considerations for all joint ventures is how the profit is split. There are several ways this can be done. The most common split is 50 / 50 where each party gets 50% of all profits. Another split might see one partner getting all the cash flow and then sharing in the profits at the time of the sale.

Joint Venture Agreement

The key to a good joint venture is a well-documented *Joint Venture Agreement*. The agreement must specify what each party's responsibility is and what each party's expected profits will be and when they will receive their proceeds.

For example, I did a lot of joint ventures for my rent-to-own business. I was responsible for finding the tenant and qualifying them. I was responsible for finding a property for the tenant. I was responsible for managing the tenant and the property during the term of the agreement.

My joint venture partner was responsible for putting up all the money. He provided the down payment and closing costs and was also responsible for getting a mortgage for the balance of the purchase price.

Since I was managing the property, I acquired my profits from the positive monthly cash flow and received the balance of my profits at the time of the sale at the end of the term of the rent to own agreement. My money partner usually only received his profits at the time of the sale. Many of my partners liked this because they were able to defer this income until the final closing and sale of the property to the tenant buyer, which was usually after three years.

You can have a different Joint Venture Agreement for each project that you have with a specific joint venture partner, or you can have one joint venture agreement that covers all deals with that same partner. I have done it both ways. All you have to do is amend the agreement to include each new property.

Joint ventures can be a good passive investment for the money partner as long as they get the right experienced real estate partner.

5.4 – Ten Mistakes Beginner Real Estate Investors Make

Real estate investing is harder than you think. Consequently, most people don't make money as a real estate investor. I have had many investors come to me for advice or have asked me to take over their property for them. They are fed up with tenants, toilets and trash. They have had too many issues that they never planned for or ever wanted to deal with. They were hoping for a passive investment — but instead, all they got was a big headache!

Here are 10 common mistakes beginner real estate investors make:

1. Lack of a Plan

> ***The first thing you need to do before you start investing in real estate is come up with a plan.***

The plan doesn't have to be a big 50-page business document, it just needs to cover a few basic points. For example, what type of real estate investing will you focus on? How will you finance your investments?

This type of planning will help determine a lot of your marketing and activities that you will be doing in your real estate investing business. For example, you won't be advertising for any tenants if you are following the fix and flip strategy.

You must always have a plan when starting your real estate investing business — even if it's a simple one.

2. Getting Lousy Financing

Most people don't realize that they can shop around for their mortgage financing.

> ***The key to getting good, affordable mortgage financing, is to have a good mortgage broker.***

A good mortgage broker will have access to a lot of lenders with many different products. Rather than shop around for a good mortgage, many people just go to the bank that they have been dealing with for years and ask for a mortgage to purchase their investment property. I have seen people pay 1% to 3% more for their financing than they should have because they didn't shop around for their mortgage.

Therefore, when looking for financing for our investment property, always make sure you get a good mortgage broker who can shop around for the best rates. This could save you a lot in your overall financing plus help with your monthly cash flow.

3. Doing Everything Yourself

When I first started investing, I thought I could do everything myself. I wrote up my own contracts, made my own offers, negotiated everything myself and even managed all my properties. I later realized that I made a lot of costly mistakes that I could have avoided by just hiring the right people to do the job. For example, I did a poor job of managing my own properties and should have hired a property manager.

> ***So, if you want to do well as a real estate investor, I recommend you get help from the experts.***

You want to spend most of your time finding and negotiating deals.

You should always use a Realtor to conduct all your purchases and sales. You will also need a good lawyer to write up your contracts and to perform all your buying and selling transactions. A good accountant will save you lots of money by showing you how to set up your deals properly. In addition, make sure you hire yourself a good property manager.

4. Overpaying When You Buy

In a seller's market, people tend to pay more for a property. As a new investor, you may get frustrated and pay too much for a property because you are trying to get a deal done. When looking for a property, don't become impatient. You need to persist until you find the right property that meets your requirements. It's a numbers game. The protocol is to look at 100 properties, analyze 10 of them, make an offer on three and purchase one. There is an expression in real estate that states, *"You make your money when you buy"*. Therefore, make sure that you don't overpay for your properties and that you stay patient and wait for the right deal to come along.

5. Underestimating Expenses / Costs

When evaluating a property, make sure you take into account all the expenses.

For example. in the case of a buy-rent-and-hold investment, you are expected to allocate a percentage for property management, a percentage for maintenance and a percentage for vacancy allowance, when estimating expenses. These are often the expenses many sellers will leave out to make the rental investment look better than it actually is.

In the case of fix and flip investments, make sure you include carrying costs in your estimates. These are the costs you will incur when your property doesn't sell as fast as you thought it would.

6. Thinking Get Rich Quick

> ***A lot of people get into real estate because they think it is a get rich quick venture.***

These people start out fast, try to learn as fast as possible, read a few books, then go out and acquire a property. Afterward, they find out they did a few things wrong. They would usually miscalculate expenses and therefore, find themselves owning a property that has a negative cash flow. In other instances, they end up realizing they did not qualify a tenant properly, so now they regret having to deal with that dreaded 'bad tenant' in their property. A bad tenant is much worse than an empty unit. This is where property owners have no choice but to study the landlord-tenant rules that apply in their respective areas.

7. Renting to Anyone

If you have an empty property the best thing you can do is rent it out, right? Wrong.

> ***Before you rent out your property, you want to make sure you qualify your tenant.***

To property qualify a potential tenant, you want to start by doing reference checks. You want to do a proper credit check on every potential tenant. You want to make sure that they have the necessary rents and deposits. Some areas allow for first and last month's rents and damage deposits. An empty property is a lot better than a bad tenant. I have had one bad tenant that cost me $30,000 in damages and another one that cost me about the same amount in missed rents.

8. Listening to the Wrong People

It always amazes me how some people can start marketing themselves as coaches after having done only a couple of real estate transactions. It seems to be a common theme in real estate investing. You do a couple of deals and then go and make money by teaching other people how to do what you now know, which isn't really a lot.

> ***The problem with most of the people coaching real estate investing is that they don't have enough experience to properly coach YOU.***

These so-called coaches might have good intentions, but they have not experienced the same problems that you may encounter. They haven't seen enough deals or had enough real-world experience yet to know how to respond to all your problems.

9. Buying for Appreciation

I have seen some people purchase rental properties strictly for appreciation. Their expenses exceed their rental income but they still purchase the property anyway. They reason that it's hard to find a positive cash-flowing property in their neighborhood.

> ***You should never buy a rental property strictly based on appreciation.***

What happens if the property doesn't appreciate as planned? At the very least, you should make sure that your expenses are covered by your rental incomes. You will always make money from the mortgage principal being paid down every month. That is about the only profit you are guaranteed from a rental property, as long as the tenant keeps paying the rent.

10. Being Too Emotional

Real estate investing is a business and should be treated as one.

You should never buy an investment property based on emotions.

You should never make any renovations based on personal preferences. As a businessperson, you do not want to get emotionally involved with a property or with a tenant.

When we first started our rental business, we heard all kinds of stories from our tenants. There were even a few times where I took pity on the tenants and conceded to their requests, allowing them to pay their rents late or pay less than the rental amount. The problem with this is the tenant will now start to think you're soft and they will start taking advantage of you, as was the case with several of our tenants early on in my rental business.

So, there you have a list of some of the common mistakes beginner real estate investors make.

CHAPTER 6

Passive Investing for Busy People

There are several reasons why people are looking for passive investments. The first reason, and probably the biggest reason, is that it is what most people are used to. If you are used to letting a financial advisor manage your investment portfolio, then you are probably a very passive investor. All you ever did was contact your financial advisor and they would come up with a strategy to invest your money into stocks, bonds, and mutual funds.

People are conditioned to be passive investors so they are looking to real estate to provide them with a similar passive investment. However, being a passive real estate investor can be hard if you don't know what you are doing. Furthermore, most people buy the wrong real estate investment to support their passive investment goals.

So, you might ask, what does passive investment really mean?

> ***There are several things that you should be looking for when looking for a passive real estate investment.***

Passive investing does not mean you should give up control of your investments either. This is how a lot of people were managing their investment portfolios. They would invest a bunch of money with their investment advisor and check with them every year or so to see how things were doing. And if their investment wasn't doing very well, their investment advisor would explain that the market was down, but it should turn around soon.

The other piece of advice that investment advisors are famous for giving is to suggest to their investors to buy more of the same investment after the stock has fallen in price. Since the investment is now priced lower, the investor would be able to buy more of the same investment at a much better price. This is called *dollar-cost averaging.*

The other reason why people are looking for passive investments is that they are busy. The majority of people lead busy lives. They are busy with their families or they are busy with their careers or both. They do not have time to spend learning about a company to invest in or to learn all about a particular real estate investment strategy. Real estate investing can be a lot of work. However, there are some real estate investing strategies that are very passive. You just need to know where to look.

Passive investing is not for people who are learning to become an active real estate investor. Passive investing is for people who have a substantial amount of capital that they can lend to others or use to become a money partner in some joint ventures. The amount of money that a passive investor should invest in real estate can vary considerably depending on your available cash, your age, and your goals.

The earlier you start your investing, the less capital you need and the less money you have to save monthly or annually. For example, someone starting their passive real estate investment strategy at age 25 could start with as little as $15,000, while someone starting at age 45 may need $100,000 or more, depending on the person's investment and retirement goals.

6.1 - What Is Passive Investing

Passive investing can mean many things to different people. People like the thought of real estate investing because they think they can quit their day job and replace their income with real estate investing. Nothing could be further from the truth.

Investing in Real Estate can be very time consuming, especially if you have never done it before and you have to learn everything while actually doing it. That's how I learned.

People are often misled or misinformed about what real estate investing can do for them. For example, buying rental properties is a long-term strategy and does not provide a good enough source of income to replace their current salary.

People often think they can buy a rental property and use the rents to replace their income. The problem with rentals is that there is barely enough cash flow to cover all the expenses associated with owning real estate. You have to take into consideration the mortgage payment, taxes, insurance, maintenance, repairs, management, etc.

> ***True passive investing is where you invest your money and you earn a return on that money, without any further involvement on your part.***

Most people get into real estate investing, not because they like real estate, but because they are seeking out alternative means of making money. Moreover, most people are not looking to make money just for the sake of making money; rather, they are motivated by what money can do for them.

These wants or desires can be viewed as a hierarchy of desires with the top being the ultimate desire and the levels below representing the steps required to achieve the ultimate desire. Here is an example of what I think this hierarchy of desires could look like with real estate at the lowest level.

Hierarchy of Desires

Dreams:	Time with family. Things to have. Things to do. Traveling.
Survival:	Care for family. Care for aging parents. Shelter. Food.
Money:	Income. Savings. Retirement Fund.
Strategy:	Real Estate Investing. Other investments

What people don't realize is that the type of real estate investment strategy that they chose may require a lot of work and a lot of knowledge. It also requires a lot of discipline, perseverance and time.

Real Estate Investing is not a get rich type of investment.

Real Estate Investing is not like investing in some hot new stock that takes the market by storm. It's also not as if you're contributing to the next killer internet solution that is going to be bought by Google.

There are many ways to make money in real estate.

Some real estate investment strategies require more work than others. Usually, the more you are involved, the higher the return on your investment but the riskier the investment is. Fix and flips may require a lot of work but they have the potential to make the most money and the potential to lose the most money. What all of this amounts to is the typical risk versus reward scenario.

When people think of passive investing, they are thinking about exchanging their 9-5 job for something that will provide them with a means to earn an income without having to exchange time for money. They want a truly passive investment.

> ***What may seem like a passive investment on the surface, may require more work than you think.***

For example, I was speaking with someone the other day who was a silent investor in a fix and flip investment. The project ran into a problem and the "passive investor" ended up having to take over the project and spend a lot more money than was originally anticipated. Consequently, he had to spend a lot of time to get the project back on track.

> ***If done correctly, real passive investing is supposed to be boring. If done correctly, passive real estate investing is consistent.***

However, people are looking for the get rich quick investment instead of the consistent and boring one.

The type of real estate investment you choose should also be based on a number of different variables. Age, real estate experience, other investment holdings, source of funds, geographical area, net worth, etc. are all factors that you will need to consider when looking for a passive real estate investment.

Risk is another big consideration when looking for passive investments. The higher the expected return often means the higher the risk.

> ***But risk tolerance varies from person to person.***

The same criteria used to determine the suitability of a passive investment for you should also include the *degree of risk* that you are most comfortable with.

For example, the older you are, usually mean that it is less likely you will want to take chances with your money.

There is also a lot of talk around diversification and how to diversify your investment portfolio.

Investment experts are always saying to diversify your investments. They then tell you to put all your money into the stock market, yet at the same token, they recommend that you divide your investment into different sectors within the stock market.

> ***Adding real estate to your portfolio provides diversification as a separate asset class.***

You can also diversify within the real estate asset class by using different real estate investment strategies or different real estate projects.

For example, you can invest in rental properties, fix and flip projects, development projects, lease option properties, wholesaling deals, private mortgages, equity investments, etc.

Don't worry. As a passive investor, all you have to decide is which real estate investment is right for you and then find ways to invest in that strategy.

> ***The key to making money as a passive real estate investor is to invest with an expert and with someone you can trust.***

In real estate investing, there are a lot of people giving out advice. They think that completing a couple of deals qualifies them as experts. It has been said that to be an expert in any subject, you need to put in about 10,000 hours of progressive learning into that subject. This amounts to about 5 years of full-time studying at approximately 2,000 hours per year learning that subject. If you were to do it part-time, at about half as much time, it would take you 10 years.

"Put all your eggs in one basket and watch that basket"

— Andrew Carnegie

That's how I think about investing in real estate. I diversify within real estate by investing in multiple strategies, multiple projects, and engaging mostly in passive investments.

The majority of investment options out there are passive anyway so there is nothing 'new' with passive real estate investing. Stocks and bonds, mutual funds, gold, silver, among others are all regarded as passive investments. People generally expect that to be a real estate investor, you need to learn how to become an *active* investor. This is not true.

There is a multitude of ways to get started as a real estate investor that doesn't require you to have any money. However, none of these options are passive investment strategies.

Another common theme in real estate investing is that you can get started without using any of your own money. This is true for most *active* investors.

Passive investment requires that you have money to invest.

The main idea with passive investing is that you invest your money and your money will subsequently work for you over time. You are not exchanging time for money like you are doing while earning a salary or as an active real estate investor.

Of course, there is nothing stopping you from using real estate to make money initially, as an active investor, and then invest your earned money into a passive investment later on.

6.2 - How to Evaluate a Passive Real Estate Investment

All passive real estate investments are not equal.

There are many different types of real estate investments. You can get involved in real estate as a passive investor in many different ways. The challenge with wanting to be a passive investor is that, since you don't want to be involved in the investment you have to make sure that you do your due diligence when selecting an investment.

There are certain things that you will need to take into consideration when evaluating a passive investment.

How Passive Do You Want to Be?

There are many different levels of passiveness that you can achieve when looking for passive investments. Some people would like to see their investment and visit the job site every now and then. I had one investor who would drive by his investment property about once a month and send me a note telling me the property is still there and everything looks good.

> ***Other people are just as happy to write a check and wait for the project to be completed or for the investment to mature.***

How passive of an investment will depend on how involved you want to be.

- Do you want regular updates on the project?
- How frequently do you want these updates?
- Do you want to be involved in the decision-making process?
- Do you want to be on title or just a cash investor?

Location of the Investment

There may be some consideration for wanting the investment property to be closer to you.

The main advantage of investing in a property close to you is that if something goes wrong with the investment, you can always go visit the property. This is where you want to become more active if something happens and the project gets in trouble.

That being said, some people just like to have the investment close by so they can drive by and check things out every now and then. The disadvantage of wanting your investment property closer to you is that there may not be as many good investment opportunities for you in your own local market.

> ***If you invest with someone you trust and you are happy being totally passive, then location should not be an issue for you.***

Experience of a Team

You will want to make sure that you are dealing with people who have experience in the type of project you are investing in. Sure, it's good to invest with friends and family, but a lot of relationships have gone bad as a result of failed projects from an inexperienced friend or family member.

When trying to determine the level of experience someone has, you will want to ask these types of questions:

- How many **years** of experience do they have?
- How many **projects** of this type have they successfully completed?
- Do they have any **references** that they can provide?

For example, most first-time fix and flip investments fail because people:

- Underestimate the cost of the materials
- Underestimate the amount of work that needs to be done
- Underestimate the amount of time it takes to do the work
- Underestimate the amount of time it takes to sell the property
- Overestimate the selling price of the finished product

Therefore, when looking for someone to invest with, make sure this is not their first project of this type, and that they have a proven track record that shows they are successful at this type of investment.

Ownership of Investment

What type of ownership of the investment are you looking to have?

> ***Some people want to be 100% owner of the property when they get into a joint venture and they want to remain 100% owner for the life of the project.***

To be 100% owner would require that you, the investor, purchase the property with all cash or with the help of a mortgage. Furthermore, this means that you would have to get qualified by a lender to be able to obtain a mortgage.

Conversely, maybe you just want to provide your cash and stay off the title of the property. In this case, your property should be secured by a mortgage charge against the investment property, where you are the mortgage holder.

These types of investments are usually secured by a Promissory Note or Private Mortgage.

Real Estate Investment Strategy

There are many different real estate investment strategies that you can choose from. In addition, your choice should depend on what excites you or interests you. Maybe you like the thought of fixing something. Maybe you like the idea of owning properties for the long haul.

Each real estate investment strategy brings with it different types of risk and different degrees of risk.

Here are a few real estate investment strategies. We will look at these based on risk, time, passiveness, capital required and return expected.

Buy, Rent and Hold

Buy, rent and hold strategy is simply buying a property and renting it out.

You might choose a buy rent and hold strategy because you are familiar with this business model. Moreover, you may know where the property is and you might be able to go see it often if it is located in your city. Rentals have been around a long time and there are a lot of regulations around rentals.

Risk	Time	Active	Capital	Return
Low	10+ years	Medium	Medium	Medium

Property Development

You may choose this strategy because you like the thought of building something and contributing to the community. Property development comes with its own set of risks and rewards. Make sure you choose an experienced developer to work with.

Risk	Time	Active	Capital	Return
Medium	1+ year	High	High	High

Fix and Flip - Single Family Home

This is where you buy a property, fix it up and sell it at a higher price that will cover all your costs such that you end up with some money left over to make a profit. People tend to like fix and flips.

Fix and flips are very popular on TV. However, if you don't know what you are doing, these real estate transactions can be very risky. There is a tendency on television to only show the projects that are successful.

Risk	Time	Active	Capital	Return
High	6+ month	High	High	High

Mortgage Lender - Private

Mortgage investing is where you lend money to an owner at a fixed rate of return. It's like you are acting as a bank.

The loan is secured through a mortgage charge on a property that operates as security. The loan could be a mortgage in any position (i.e. first, second, third, etc.) which basically identifies the position of the mortgage at the time it is registered on title. For example, if you go ahead and register a loan on the title and there is already one registered, then the position of that loan is second.

Risk	Time	Active	Capital	Return
Low	1+ years	Low	Low	Medium

Private placement investment Lender

A private placement investment is where a corporation raises money for a large development such as large apartment complexes. The money is raised through an exempt market dealer who is licensed to raise money for companies that have been granted a prospectus exemption. This means they can raise money without having to go public and without having their company registered as a public company on the stock exchange.

Risk	Time	Active	Capital	Return
Low	2+ years	None	Low-High	Medium

REITs / MICs

A Real Estate Investment Trust (REIT) is a trust designed to invest in real estate for the purposes of making money. The trust would typically own several properties and the money earned on these investments is used to pay the investors.

A Mortgage Investment Corporation (MIC) is an organization set up to lend money to individuals or corporations for the purpose of purchasing real estate. This is very similar to how banks and other lenders lend out money. The big difference is that MICs are funded through investments of other people's money.

A MIC earns its money through payments made by the borrowers and in turn, uses the accumulated payments to pay back its investors.

Investing in a REIT and MIC is very similar to simply investing in stocks.

Risk	Time	Active	Capital	Return
Low	3+ years	None	Low-High	Low

Summary

There you have a summary of the more common ways in which you can become a Real Estate Investor and how you would evaluate which investment is right for you.

6.3 - The Biggest Lie in Real Estate Investing

The biggest lie in real estate investing is that you can buy several rental properties and earn enough income to replace your day job.

This lie has been told to people in order to entice them to buy investment properties as rentals. I'm not sure how such a strategy has been misrepresented for so long, but it certainly has. I have read it in many books. I have seen it being pushed by many investment clubs and by many experienced investors. However, I constantly see people struggle with this strategy and these people never achieve their original goal of replacing their income with rental properties. More often than not, they don't achieve their objective for quite a few years.

The simple premise is that you buy a property and rent it out. The difference between what you collect in rental income and the expenses is your cash flow. For example, assume you buy a property for $300,000 and you rent it out for $2,000. Next, assume you have mortgage payments of $1,300, a property tax expense of $300 per month and property insurance of $100 per month. Your total expenses would add up to $1,700. Therefore, your cash flow is $300 a month. If you have 10 rental properties, your positive cash flow is $3,000 a month or $36,000 a year. A nice profit, right? Wrong! This will never happen.

The problem with this example is that it does not include all of the other expenses. Properties need to be managed and they need to be maintained. Furthermore, you also need to take into account a vacancy allowance.

When estimating your cash flow, you need to add in estimates for 1) vacancy 2) property management and 3) repairs and maintenance. I normally include about 5% of the gross rents for each of these. Depending on the property, it may be more or it may be less. It could be less for a newer property in a good neighborhood. It would definitely be more for an older property in a poor neighborhood.

Using our example above the calculation now looks like this:

$2,000	Gross Rent
$1,300	Mortgage Payment
$ 300	Tax Payment
$ 100	Insurance Payment
$ 100	5% Property Management Allowance
$ 100	5% Maintenance and Repairs
$ 100	5% Vacancy Allowance
$2,000	Total Expenses

With this revised example, your net cash flow is now $0. An overwhelming majority of people don't factor in the estimates for property management, maintenance and repairs, and vacancy. They would often say they will do the work themselves. If that's the case, then they are really opting to work for free. However, you still can't avoid the costs for materials in your maintenance costs.

Other big expenses can occur if you have to replace or fix a major item such as windows, furnace, roof, etc. Furthermore, what if you have a very bad tenant who destroys the place and it takes forever to evict them? You would then have the cost of repairing the damage the tenant has caused, in addition to the lost rent if the tenant has stopped paying. Not to mention the additional lost rent while you are repairing the property after the tenant is gone!

The other reason people don't add these additional expenses into their estimates is that they are anxious to get a deal done and they are tired of looking around for a property to invest in. I know that that's what happened to me with my first deal. People will sometimes say that there are not any properties that will cash flow in their area, which actually may be the case. Thus, they leave out these major expenses in their estimates just so it looks like the property will have a positive cash flow, at least on paper. They are playing some kind of psychological game with themselves.

One of the most misrepresented property indicators is the *Cap Rate*. The Cap Rate or *Capitalization Rate* is a number that shows a ratio of net revenues to price, exclusive of financing. The reason this is so misleading is that everyone calculates it differently. The actual formula is this:

Cap Rate = Annual Net Income / House Price x 100%
Net Income = Gross Rental Income - Expenses

So, in our example above, the Cap Rate would be calculated as follows:

Net Income = $2,000 - $700 (mortgage not included) = $1,300 x 12 = $15,600
Cap Rate = $15,600 / $300,000 x 100% = **5.2%**

The problem is that most people leave out the management, maintenance and vacancy expenses when calculating Cap Rate, which thereby makes the Cap Rate look much better than it actually is. If they DID leave out those expenses, their calculation would be:

Net Income = $2,000 - $400 (mortgage not included) = $1,600 x 12 = $19,200
Cap Rate = $19,200 / $300,00 x 100% = **6.4%**

Now the Cap Rate looks much better than it actually is. The real problem is that the calculation of the Cap Rate is inconsistent and hard to compare from one project to another.

Other people understand that there will be no cash flow, and they are strictly buying for appreciation and equity growth and that's OK. Just as long as they realize that, there is no short-term positive cash flow with their properties and that their properties may not appreciate.

Money is made with real estate rentals in 3 different ways.

1. **Monthly Cash Flow** - We already covered this. On newer homes, with no repairs, it might still be possible to make a small positive cash

flow but I would not count on it. Again, rentals should not be purchased for cash flow.

2. **Mortgage Principal Pay Down** - Every time you make a mortgage payment, you are paying down a portion of the original mortgage. This means that you are building up equity. This is the only guaranteed profit in real estate. But sometimes, you may have to refinance your property and pull the equity out to fix a major item on your property.

3. **Property Appreciation** - This is the value of the property that may increase over several years. However, this is also not guaranteed and I have actually bought properties that have decreased in value. In some cases, you may be able to force appreciation by increasing the value of the home. For example, adding an in-law suite may increase the value of the home.

Investing in rental properties is a long-term strategy that requires purchasing multiple properties over a long period of time.

For example, the plan might be that you buy 10 properties and then rent them out for ten years. Unfortunately, you don't make much profit for those properties during those ten years based on all the reasons I just went over previously. After 10 years, you sell off 5 of your properties and use the profits from those 5 properties to pay off the remaining 5 that you still have. Finally, you have 5 properties without any mortgage which will give you nice positive cash flow. Plus, your rents most likely would have gone up during that time period.

Using our example above, the calculation now looks like this:

$2,400 Gross Rent (assuming 2% rent increase per year)

$ 0 Mortgage Payment
$ 300 Tax Payment

$ 100	Insurance Payment
$ 100	5% Property Management Allowance
$ 100	5% Maintenance and Repairs
$ 100	5% Vacancy Allowance
$ 700	Total Expenses

This time around, your net cash flow is $1,700 per property. If you have 5 properties left, your total monthly positive cash flow is now $8,500 per month or $102,000 per year. Now, you can quit your day job!

In conclusion, when looking to invest in rental properties, it is important to know that there will be no monthly cash flow for a number of years.

Single-family home rentals are a long-term investment strategy.

CHAPTER 7

Passive Investing with Mortgages

Probably the easiest and least used real estate investment strategy is mortgage investing. This strategy is not used by the average investor. The reason you don't hear a lot about mortgage investing is that most people who get into real estate investing are looking to own properties. They are focused on *the allure of real estate investing*. There seems to be some sort of prestige with owning properties. People like to talk about the fact that they physically own real estate. It gives them a feeling of importance. Nowadays, I do not own any real estate but I have owned over 60 properties at one point of time in my career.

I was at a real estate investing seminar the other day and this lady came up to me and asked me for some help. She told me that she wanted to buy a triplex. I asked her why she wanted to buy a triplex since I wanted to figure out how this purchase would align with her goals. She couldn't really answer me other than to say that she just simply wanted to own a triplex.

Another reason you don't hear a lot about mortgage investing is that it is boring. It's as simple as you lending money to someone and they pay you interest on that loan. After a specified length of time, they pay you back the original loan principal. During that time, you continue to earn interest until the loan is fully paid off.

Another reason why you do not hear a lot about mortgage investing is that the majority of real estate professionals are motivated to sell you a property. They aren't really interested in your money other than for a down payment to purchase a property.

> ***It's very easy to get started with Mortgage investing. All you need is the cash, a property to lend against and a lawyer to conduct the transaction.***

The best place to find mortgage investments is through a licensed mortgage broker. Mortgage brokers are in the business of finding money for people who need money and then securing the loan by issuing a mortgage. Commonly, the mortgage broker gets the money from institutional lenders: mainly banks and other companies who specialize in lending. However, there is also the occasion where a mortgage broker will need to find money from private lenders because the borrower will be considered too risky for the institutional lender.

As a mortgage investor, you are lending money to an individual or company just like the banks lend money. Your money is secured against a property by a charge against that property, otherwise known as a mortgage.

Mortgage investing may seem risky at first because you are lending money to someone that the banks won't lend to. However, commercial banks have the tendency to be ultra-conservative and only lend money to people with good to excellent credit and who have higher incomes. If you are OK with taking a little bit of risk you can make a lot of money in mortgage investing. Moreover, mortgage investing is not as risky as you think. The main reason it's not that risky is that it is still secured by real estate, so if the borrower stops paying the mortgage payments, you can always foreclose on him and you end up with the property as a result

7.1 - What is a Mortgage Investment

Mortgage investments are some of the most passive investment of all real estate investment strategies. When you invest in mortgages, you are basically acting like a bank and you are loaning someone the money to purchase a property or to build a new home. But, instead of the bank as the lender, YOU are the lender. The property owner is still the borrower. There could be another mortgage on the property that you are lending money against. That other mortgage would usually be from a bank or another financial institution.

What is a Mortgage (as defined in Investopedia)?

> *A mortgage is a debt instrument, secured by the collateral of specified real estate property, that the borrower is obliged to pay back with a predetermined set of payments. Mortgages are used by individuals and businesses to make large real estate purchases without paying the entire value of the purchase up front. Over a period of many years, the borrower repays the loan, plus interest, until he/she eventually owns the property free and clear. Mortgages are also known as "liens against property" or "claims on property." If the borrower stops paying the mortgage, the lender can foreclose.*

Mortgage Interest Rates

Lenders will usually charge a rate of interest when lending money to a borrower. However, I have seen situations where lenders have loaned people money at 0% interest to help finalize the sale of their own property. This is commonly known as a Vendor Take Back mortgage or VTB mortgage. This is not a mortgage investment. This is a tool the owner used to facilitate the sale of their home. However, it is still a mortgage with 0% interest. In this scenario, it's possible for the owner to get full price, so he made his money that way and didn't have to charge interest.

If interest is charged, it can be calculated in many different ways. That calculation will determine how much the borrower has to pay every month. Monthly is the most common term, but other terms, such as weekly or even annually, are also possible.

The interest calculation will be based on the original loan amount, the interest rate charged, the amortization period and the payment frequency. I won't go into the details here, as there are many calculators available online where you can see the effects of these variables. Interest rates can be either **variable**, commonly referred to as adjustable-rate mortgage (ARM) or **fixed**. Mortgages can also be **blended** or **interest only**.

A variable rate mortgage from a bank will fluctuate with the bank's prime rate throughout the mortgage term. While your regular payment will remain constant, your interest rate may change based on market conditions. This impacts the amount of principal you pay off each month but not your payment amount. When rates on variable interest rate mortgages decrease, more of your regular payment is applied to your principal. Additionally, if rates increase, more of your payment will go toward the interest.

Open variable rate mortgages usually offer an option to convert the mortgage to a fixed-rate closed mortgage at any time, without a prepayment penalty. Variable-rate interest rates are usually lower than fixed-rate mortgages. People borrowing on variable rate terms are usually hoping that interest rates will remain low for the short term. They are protected because they have the right to convert to a fixed-rate mortgage at any time.

Fixed-rate mortgages have the same rate of interest throughout the term of the mortgage. People who borrow on fixed-rate terms are protected knowing they will be locked in at a set interest rate and payment amount and are not subject to variations in the bank's prime rate, like with variable-rate mortgages.

Blended mortgage payments are comprised of a principal portion and an interest portion. That means that every time a mortgage payment is made, a portion of the payment goes towards paying the interest and a portion of the payment goes towards paying the principal of the original mortgage loan, thus reducing the original loan amount.

For example, if John has a mortgage payment of $600 a month, the first payment he makes may comprise of $590 interest and $10 principal, thus reducing the amount of the loan by only $10. This blended split of interest and principal will change with every payment as each payment lowers the principal owing, thus reducing the amount of interest paid and increasing the amount of principal paid. At the end of the mortgage term, the borrower owes an amount less than the original amount. In Canada, by law, all blended fixed mortgages are compounded semi-annually.

An **interest-only** mortgage uses the simple interest to calculate the payment and does not reduce the original loan amount.

For example, if John borrows $30,000 at a rate of 10% annually, interest only, his monthly payments will be $30,000 x 10% = $3,000 annually / 12= $250 per month. John will pay $250 per month for the term of the mortgage, assuming the mortgage payments are monthly. These payments do not contain a principal amount as they are interest only. Therefore, these payments do not reduce the amount of the loan. At the end of the term, John still owes $30,000. Most mortgage investments are calculated using simple interest only.

People can invest in mortgages in different ways. The most common way is as a private mortgage lender. This is where an individual, or company, lends money to another individual or company. That loan is secured by registering a mortgage against the property.

There are several things to consider when looking to invest in mortgages:

1. **Loan to Value** - What is the loan to value of all mortgages registered against the property? The loan to value is the percentage of the sum of all the mortgage loans relative to the actual value of the property. The higher the loan to value percentage, the riskier the investment and therefore, the higher the interest the lender will charge.

2. **Borrower's Capability** - You want to make sure that the borrower has good credit and a good history of paying back their loans. You will want to perform a credit check on individual borrowers and you will probably want to ask for proof of income including their latest tax filings. Your mortgage broker can arrange for all of that.

3. **Interest Rates** - The higher the risk, the higher the interest rate should be. Also, if there are multiple mortgages, the higher the position, the higher the interest rate. For example, if there are three mortgages showing on the property and yours is the third, it should carry the highest interest rate — since it's the riskiest of the three. Whenever a house is sold, it pays out the mortgages in the order they are registered on title. Therefore, a third mortgage only gets paid third, which may be a problem if the property sale did not get enough to cover the amount owed to all mortgages.

4. **Type of Project** - Is it a single-family home? A condo development? An apartment building? Commercial property? Land? Typically, residential mortgages are safer than commercial mortgages and the terms are better as well.

5. **Location, Location, Location** - Where is the property located? Is it in a good part of town or is it in a bad part of town? Is it located in the city or is it located in the suburbs or even the country for that matter? Personally, I wouldn't lend money for a property in the country. There are not as many buyers so it would be hard to recover the loan if I ever had to foreclose on the borrower. You want to lend to people

with properties in major communities where there is a higher demand for homes in that area.

In summary, mortgage investing is a good passive way to invest in real estate. Just make sure you do your analysis before investing.

7.2 – Investing in Private Mortgages

Private mortgage investing is when an individual or company, lends another individual or company money. This loan is then secured through a charge on a particular piece of real estate. That charge is called a mortgage. It is referred to as private because there is no financial institution involved. It is still public in the sense anyone can ask for a title search and see that there is a mortgage registered on the property. This registration prevents the owner from selling the house without paying the money that was borrowed, by using the property as collateral.

All mortgages, whether they are private or not, are usually referred to as either first, second, or third mortgages (and beyond). The number (first, second, etc.) indicates when the mortgage was registered against the title of the property and indicates when the mortgage would be paid if the property is sold.

A **first mortgage** is a loan secured by the property that is in first or "senior" position and gets paid first if the property is sold (municipal liens like property taxes are TRULY first, though). This is important to know as a property could be sold for non-payment of taxes.

A **second mortgage** is a loan that has a "junior" or subordinate position behind a first mortgage and is paid after the first mortgage and any municipal liens. Technically you can have 3rd, 4th, 5th, etc. mortgages.

It is very common for Private Mortgages to be in second, third or positions further down the line. It is not so common to have Private Mortgages in the first position since this is where the banks have their stake. Banks will always want to be in the first position.

First mortgage loans are the least risky and therefore usually carry the lowest interest rate because it gets paid first. Banks or financial institutions are the most common lenders of first mortgage loans. If you are investing in first mortgages it is because the bank has not approved the borrower and the borrowers are looking for private financing. Interest rates for private first mortgage loans are usually significantly higher than bank-provided mortgage loans. For example, at the time of this writing, bank-provided first mortgage loans are charging a rate of approximately 3% for a three-year closed mortgage. Private first mortgage rates are around 7%, for the same term.

Second mortgages and all other subordinate mortgages are riskier and usually carry a higher interest rate to reflect that additional risk. For example, current private second mortgage rates are around 10% to 12%. There are usually additional setup fees charged to the borrower to set up the mortgage. That means that the lender will charge another 2% or 3% just to set up the mortgage loan. For example, if the loan is $50,000, there could also be an additional $1,500 charged, if the setup fee was 3%. As an investor, you should always charge these fees.

If a mortgage broker is involved, they will also want to charge a fee of between 2% to 3%. Thus, the total setup fee a borrower would have to pay could be as high as 6%. This is a very common practice in private mortgages but most borrowers do not mind. There is an expression in real estate investing:

The cost of money is not as important as access to that money.

That means that the borrowers don't mind paying the high interest rates and the setup fees as long as they can get approved for the financing.

When investing in private mortgages, make sure you do your due diligence.

There are a few things you need to consider before becoming a private mortgage investor and start lending your money.

1. **Borrower** - Always examine the borrower's capabilities. This means you should review their credit report and their income. You want to

make sure the borrower's income is sufficient to cover all mortgages and all debt payments.

2. **Property** - Check out the property to make sure it is worth what the borrower is saying it is worth. This usually requires getting an appraisal from a registered appraiser. You want to make sure there is enough equity in the home to pay you should you be required to sell the property if the borrower ever defaults. You also want to make sure that the property is located in a desirable neighborhood so it sells fast.

3. **Loan to Value (LTV)** - The loan to value is the ratio of all loans to the value of the house and is expressed as a percentage:

   Amount of Loans / Value of House x 100% = LTV

   The value is usually determined by the appraisal. Most private mortgage lenders will not exceed 80% LTV. This means that the total value of all loans should not exceed 80%.

   For example, if the house being mortgaged is worth $300,000, the total loans should only be $240,000. If there is already a first mortgage in place for $200,000, you should not loan more than $40,000. I have seen higher loan-to-values, but the interest rates increase considerably. Higher LTVs are common when you have 3rd and 4th position mortgages as well. However, beware, since you are now getting into some serious risk.

4. **Title search** - Before lending money as a mortgage, always make sure a title search is done. It may be the case that there are other mortgages or liens on the property that the lender has either purposefully neglected to tell you about or wasn't even aware of their existence. I have seen this many times where the owner has an unpaid bill, such as a construction lien, that they did not know had been registered as a lien on the title.

5. **Legal Advice** - Before lending, you should always obtain legal advice from your lawyer. They would look at the overall investment and give you legal advice and identify any risks that may be involved. You will also need a lawyer to search the title and to register your investment loan on the title.

Investing in private mortgages can be very lucrative but it still has its own risks. Make sure you do your own due diligence before investing in private mortgage loans. An experienced mortgage broker can usually take care of any and all activities associated with private mortgage investments. As indicated, mortgage brokers usually charge a heavy fee for doing this, as the work involved is a lot more complicated than just getting a conventional mortgage from a bank or institution. Furthermore, the bank is the one who normally pays the mortgage brokers fee. In private mortgages, the borrower is the one paying the fee and it will be deducted from the actual loan amount.

For example, if John wants to borrow $30,000 and the mortgage broker's fee is $1,000, John would only receive $29,000 from the proceeds of the mortgage and the mortgage broker would get paid the $1,000 directly.

Summary of why you would invest in Private Mortgages:

- Private mortgage investments usually carry fixed monthly payments so they can provide a regular income stream.
- Investing in private mortgages is often less risky than investing in the stock market because they are secured by both the property and the borrower.
- As a lender, you have control over what property to invest in and who to invest with. Mortgage brokers are a good source of investment opportunities.
- You have the ability to negotiate interest rates and terms to get the best deal for you. This can be done through a mortgage broker or directly with the borrower.

- You get to invest in real estate without the hassles of owning real estate and having to manage a property and tenants. No dealing with "tenants, toilets, and trash", as the saying goes.
- You can also shelter your interest earnings since you can self-direct your RRSP to Private Mortgages.

In conclusion, Private Mortgages are a great way to invest in Real Estate. Make sure you do your due diligence and don't take too much risk.

7.3 - Funding Sources

Mortgage investments can be *funded* in many different ways. So where can the money come from to make the actual investment?

Cash

The easiest and fastest way to invest in Private Mortgages is by using cash. Of course, *cash* does not mean showing up at the borrower's house with a bag full of money. Cash is any money that is sitting in a bank account that is very liquid and can be used by simply writing a cheque or bank draft. The term *cash* is used to differentiate it from other sources of investment capital such as registered tax funds.

The big advantage of cash is that you are able to move fast and start investing in mortgages as soon as you find one of interest. A mortgage broker can approach you with a private mortgage investment opportunity and you could be invested in as little time as it takes to draw up the mortgage documents, do a simple title search and have the mortgage registered on title.

Mortgage brokers are a good source of mortgage investment opportunities. Another good source is your local real estate investment club.

Registered Funds

The next most common source of financing for mortgage investments is registered tax funds.

There are several types of registered tax funds in Canada, but the most common are the Registered Retirement Savings Program (RRSP) and the Tax-Free Savings Account (TFSA).

An RRSP is a bank account that can be set up which allows you to enjoy tax benefits on your investments. Any money deposited into an RRSP can be deducted from your earned income.

For example, if you have a marginal personal tax rate of 40% and you deposit $10,000 into your RRSP, you can reduce your taxable income by $4,000 for that year. The other advantage of an RRSP is that any money earned inside of an RRSP is not taxable. Therefore, if you have a mortgage investment where you earned $10,000 interest in a given year, you would not have to pay tax on that earned money in that year. The big advantage of this is the entire interest earned can be reinvested and compounded so you get the extra benefit from the amount you didn't have to pay tax on initially that stays in your account.

For example, if you earned $10,000 interest on a mortgage investment inside an RRSP, you could reinvest the entire $10,000. If you earned $10,000 interest on a mortgage through a *cash investment*, you would have to pay tax on that money in the year you earned it. So, if your marginal tax rate is 40% you would have to pay $4,000 and you would only have $6,000 to reinvest.

TFSA accounts work the same way as an RRSP once the money is in the account. The difference is that you don't get the tax benefits at the time of the deposit.

RRSP mortgages need to be handled by a trustee so this means you cannot respond to investment opportunities as quickly as if you were using cash as your source of funds.

There are also some government restrictions imposed on RRSPs and what you can and cannot invest in. If you are interested in investing in mortgages using your RRSP account, contact your mortgage broker and they should be able to help you out.

Borrowing the Money

One very creative way to invest in mortgages is to borrow the money. The way you make money is by creating a spread between what you pay to borrow the money and what you are earning from the mortgage investment.

For example, assume you are borrowing the money at 5% and you can invest the money at 10%. You are earning a difference of 5% without using any of your own money. Plus, you can charge a setup fee to the borrower for lending them the money. This is a very high leveraged return, which is actually providing you an infinite return on your money, since none of this money is your own money. The challenge with this strategy is finding the people to lend you the money.

The first source of people to borrow from is friends and family. People who are not getting a very good return with their current investments are usually very happy to get a 5% return on their money, especially if they trust you.

For example, assume Uncle Bill lends you $50,000. You invest that $50,000 by lending the money through a mortgage investment to John at 10%. You also charge John a 2% setup fee for the mortgage. After one year, your return on the investment with John is $5,000 + $1,000 setup fee. You pay Bill $2,500 ($50,000 x 5%) and you keep the rest. Therefore, you made $5,000 + $1,000 - $2,500 = $3,500 in the first year, just for finding this deal and without using any of your own money.

The only challenge with this approach is that the person lending you the money does not have any security because their loan is directly with you and not with the lender so they don't have the mortgage as security - you do. One way around this is to both be the lenders and have both names registered on the mortgage as co-lenders. In this case, Bill would be exposed to the complete deal, which is OK, as long as you are OK with having total transparency on the deal and with Bill knowing how much money you are making. Some investors don't want to disclose what they are making to their friends and family in fear of their friends doing future deals without them. If that's the case, I would advise getting new friends.

Home Equity Line of Credit

Another source of funds is a property you own. It always amazes me how many people are sitting on a dead asset in the form of their own home. They are very proud of the fact that they have paid off their mortgage. They are so proud, in fact, that they always list the equity in their home as an asset. But what good is that asset if it isn't earning income?

Let's say you own a home worth $400,000. You can go to just about any bank and get a home equity line of credit (HELOC) that allows you to borrow from that account for any purpose. The interest rate on those loans is very low since it is secured by real estate. At the time of this writing, let's assume you can get a HELOC at 3%. Then, what you can do is find a mortgage investment that pays 10% and borrow the money from your HELOC to invest in this mortgage.

For example, let's say you set up a HELOC for 60% of the value of your home. Thus, 60% of $400,000 is $240,000. In reality, you do not have to pay interest on this total amount. You only have to pay interest on the amount you borrow from the HELOC.

Subsequently, you borrow $50,000 from your HELOC and invest in John at 10%. After one year, you would receive $5,000 plus you get a setup fee of $1,000. At 3% interest, you only had to pay your HELOC a total of $1,500. After one year you earned $5,000 + $1,000 - $1,500 = $4,500. Your house has earned you an additional $4,500 just by leveraging the equity in your home and finding the right investment. What if you invested $100,000 or even $200,000? For some people, this is the difference between retiring and continuing to work. This is a simplistic view that did not take into account monthly payments but rather just showed annual returns.

In summary, there are several ways in which you can find money to invest in mortgages. Some of these ways don't even require you to use your own money. All it takes is a little creativity.

CHAPTER 8

Private Equity Investments

In this chapter, we will look at passive investing with private equity investments. They are securities that are being offered on the *exempt market*. Exempt Securities are also known as *Private Placement* offerings. A private placement is a security offering not found on the public stock exchange.

What is an Exempt Market?

The *exempt market* is where securities can be sold without having to generate a *prospectus*. These securities can be classified as "*prospectus exempt*". This approach can be useful for companies who need to raise money and don't want to spend the time and money to create a prospectus.

A couple of key differences between public securities offered through the stock market and investments offered through the prospectus exemptions are:

- investors do not receive regular updates about the performance of the investment or about the company selling it
- investors are not able to resell the security easily

What is an Exemption

An *exemption* is what allows a company to sell securities without providing a *prospectus*. The company is exempt from prospectus requirements and therefore requires less disclosure than a *prospectus offering*. To sell a security in the exempt market, an issuer must ensure that the investor qualifies under a specific exemption.

What is a Prospectus?

A *prospectus* is a legal document issued by companies that are offering securities for sale. Mutual funds also provide a prospectus to potential clients, which includes a description of the fund's strategies, the manager's background, the fund's fee structure, and a fund's financial statements.

There are several exemptions that are available to companies.

7 Types of Prospectus Exemptions

As an example, securities offered to the public in Ontario must be issued with a prospectus, but there are exceptions. These exemptions are called prospectus exemptions. Here is a description of these exemptions.

1. Accredited Investor Exemption

Companies can sell their securities to accredited investors. These are individuals who have:

- An individual net income before taxes of more than $200,000 in each of the two most recent calendar years with expected income of the same for the current calendar year.
- Combined spouse net income of more than $300,000 in each of the last two calendar years, with expected income of the same in the current calendar year.
- Combined spouse, or individual, financial assets of at least $1 million net, before taxes. Financial assets include cash and bank accounts, but do not include housing.
- All combined spouse, or individual net assets, including housing, of at least $5 million.

In addition to individuals, companies can also sell their securities to pension funds, charities and certain other entities under this exemption.

There is no limit on how much an accredited investor can invest.

2. Crowdfunding Exemption

The crowdfunding prospectus exemption enables Canadian companies to sell securities online through a single portal registered with the Ontario Securities Commission (OSC). This is usually available to early-stage companies.

Anyone can buy securities under this exemption but there are limits.

- *Anyone* can invest up to $2,500 per investment, but not more than $10,000 in total in a calendar year.
- An *accredited investor* can invest up to $25,000 per investment but not more than $50,000 in total in a calendar year.
- *Very large investors*, such as banks and governments, can invest any amount.

3. Existing Security Holder Exemption

Public companies listed on certain exchanges can sell securities to their existing security holders.

Investors who already have invested in the security can invest up to $15,000 in a 12-month period, or more if the investor has received advice from an investment dealer indicating that it is suitable for the investor.

4. Family, Friends and Business Associates Exemption

Allows companies to sell securities to its owners, officers, and directors or to most of their immediate family members, their close business associates, and their close personal friends.

There are no limits on how much these investors can invest under this exemption.

5. Minimum Amount Investment Exemption

Companies can sell their securities to a company, as long as the security's purchase price is at least $150,000 and is paid in full in cash.

6. Offering Memorandum Exemption

Allows companies to sell securities based on an *offering memorandum* being made available to investors. An offering memorandum is a document that outlines a company's business and affairs.

Eligible and non-eligible investors can invest under this exemption.

An eligible investor must have:

- Combined spouse or individual net assets exceeding $400,000.
- Before tax net income exceeding $75,000 in the previous two calendar years, with an expectation of the same in net income the current year.
- Combined spouse or individual net income of greater than $125,000 in the previous two calendar years, with an expectation of the same in the current year.

Limits on the amounts you can invest:

- As an eligible investor:
    - The total amount of securities purchased price for all securities purchased under this exemption in the 12 months cannot be more than $30,000.
    - For investors who are advised by a portfolio manager, investment dealer or exempt market dealer that an investment of over $30,000 is acceptable, the amount of all

securities purchased in the 12 months shall not exceed $100,000.

- *As a non-eligible investor:*
    - The investment amount of securities purchased in the last 12 months under this exemption cannot exceed $10,000.

7. Rights Offering Exemption

This is where public companies give the rights, on a pro-rata basis, to their existing security holders, to purchase additional securities.

The holders of these rights can decide whether to exercise them by paying the subscription price for these securities. There are no limits on how much investors can invest under this exemption.

Exempt Offering Document

This disclosure document provides financial and non-financial information related to the entity issuing the *exempt offering* (or in the case of a franchise offering, the franchisor) and the offering itself.

What is an Exempt Market Dealer (EMD)?

Exempt Market Dealers (EMDs) are fully registered securities dealers who engage in the business of trading in *prospectus exempt securities*, or any securities, to qualified exempt market clients.

Exempt Market Dealers are firms that have been licensed to distribute investment securities that haven't been qualified by a prospectus but are exempt from the prospectus requirement based on the rules and regulations of each province where the EMD is registered to carry on business. These investments are often referred to as *private capital* because they aren't publicly traded like other stocks and securities.

Exempt market dealers and their registered agents may serve as a dealer

- for any securities that are exempt from the prospectus
- for any securities selling to clients qualified for the purchase of exempt securities, and
- for investment funds that are either prospectus exempt or prospectus qualified

It is illegal to be in the business of selling these investments unless a firm is registered as an EMD under the securities regulation of the provinces where they are selling these investments. An EMD has regulated standards that make sure they know their investments, know their clients, carry reasonable insurance, and treat their clients "fairly, honestly, and in good faith".

Difference between Private Placements and Public Stock.

- Exempt market securities may involve a higher level of risk.
- There are no established secondary markets for exempt market securities and they are not very liquid.
- Unlike publicly traded companies, issuers of exempt market securities are not required to provide continuous disclosure to investors.
- Exempt market securities can only be sold by an EMD, or, in certain provinces, directly by an issuer under the North-Western Order, which is an exemption from registration requirements, with some conditions.

8.1 - How to Evaluate a Private Placement

If you are looking for a good passive investment for your savings plan or retirement plan, private placement investments (PPIs) may be a very good choice. When looking for a good PPI, you want to make sure that they meet certain criteria.

If you are looking for a good passive investment strategy for your savings plan or for your retirement plan, private placement investments (PPIs) can be a very good choice. There are certain things to look for when looking for a private placement investment. Make sure you do your due diligence. Here are some of the things to look for:

1. Experienced management team. Find out who the managers of the investment are and what their experience, expertise, educational background, character, and capabilities are. The people who run the investments have the greatest influence on the success or failure of a business. You want to invest with a team that has a proven successful track record at both the investment management level and at the operational level.
2. What is the use of the funds? Investors should have a general understanding of what their money will be spent on or invested in. This will provide insight into whether there is asset coverage or whether your capital will be entirely at risk. For example, if your investment is used for real estate, it is generally less risky than if it was used for working capital. You should also want to know if other capital is being raised by the company and if any of that capital has priority over yours.
3. What is the business model? You should understand what's the business of the company you are investing in. How does this business make money? In the case of real estate development, the business is

usually related to the development and sales of properties or the renting of them.

4. Clear investment premise. Make sure you know and understand how the company makes a profit. The profit model should be clear and based on sound financial principles. This model should be easy to understand.
5. What are the risks of the investment? Make sure you identify what the risks of the investment are. Every investment has risks. What are the business's plans for mitigating those risks? Are you comfortable with their plans? The risk should be reflected in the returns. The higher the risk, the higher the return.
6. Tax-efficient structure. Are there any tax benefits from the investment? Can it be included in your registered tax investments? Is the business managing their own tax obligations?
7. Audited financial statements. The business must provide regular financial statements. These statements have been audited. Has the company always provided these statements on time, as required?
8. Clearly defined commitment period. Make sure you understand how long your investment will be locked in for. Can you exit this investment? Is there a penalty for exiting the investment?
9. How is management compensated? How is the management team compensated? Are there different compensation levels before and after profits? Is management paid for raising capital or only for profits? Management fees should not increase based on the perceived value of the asset before it is even sold. Ideally, management should only be compensated based on the success of the investment. The higher the profit, the more money you make and the more money management makes.

Avoid exempt market risks

In general, *exempt products* have a higher risk because they have the following characteristics:

- There isn't a prospectus and their offering documents are not reviewed by the regulators and therefore don't offer the same protection to investors;
- They are not insured;
- The investment is locked in and usually not available until the investment matures;
- These investments are usually provided by smaller companies;
- These businesses are not subject to the same disclosure rules as publicly traded companies.

These risks are why these businesses are provided these exemptions and sell to more sophisticated investors who don't need the protection of a regulated public investment. However, many exempt dealers feel these exempt investments are less risky than public offerings because they are not subjected to market volatility and market fluctuations based on perception.

So, how do exempt market dealers protect their clients from the perceived risks associated with these private equity investments?

A) Suitability Evaluation

An exempt market dealer must look at each of their client's total portfolio and determine if investment in private placement investments is right for them. They will look at their client's current holdings and their diversification of those investments. Many exempt market dealers will limit how much an investor can place into private placement investments.

B) Eligibility Evaluation

An exempt market dealer must evaluate their client's financial situation to see if they are eligible to invest in a private placement offering. This includes looking at the client's net worth and income over the last 2 years. The information required to show an investor is eligible will be recorded to ensure the exempt market dealer has done their job.

(C) Product Training and Knowledge

All exempt market dealers should know the products they are selling. This allows the dealer to ensure the information provided to their clients is well described and is well understood by their clients after they have presented the offering. Exempt market dealer firms should make sure their salespeople are properly trained in all current products and provide regular training sessions to teach their dealers about any new products that have been added to the exempt market dealers list of offerings.

8.2 – Private Placement Investments versus Other Investments

Depending on what your goals are, private placement investments (PPIs) can be a great fit for you in contrast to other investments.

The two biggest criteria that you need to consider when evaluating PPIs over other investments are income and time. Subsequently, these two criteria may support or contradict each other.

Income consideration is whether or not you are looking for an income from your investment or whether you can wait for equity growth. A lot of investors are either looking to replace their income or are looking to augment their income with their investments. Other investors may be content to wait for the investment to grow and benefit from the additional equity.

Time consideration is how long can you wait for a return for your investment. Some people are looking for a return right away. They want their investment to start providing a return as soon as possible because they are looking for an income replacement. Other investors, on the other hand, may be satisfied to wait for their return over a longer period.

The following is a comparison of Private Placement Investments with some of the other real estate investment strategies:

PPIs versus Other Real Estate Investments

> ***Probably the biggest lie in real estate is that rental properties produce a regular income.***

People are told that if they buy enough properties, you can replace your current income. Rentals are a long-term investment strategy and really only provide an income after about 10 years. This is because rental properties don't really cash flow because the expenses exceed the income, in most cases.

The recommended strategy for rentals is that you buy as many properties as you can and rent them out. Over time, let's say 10 years, the mortgage gets paid down and hopefully, the properties will appreciate. After 10 years, you sell off half of your properties and use the money from the sale to pay down the rest of the properties. After you have paid down the remaining properties, you now have properties without any mortgage. This means that the remaining properties will definitely cash flow and will provide a good source of income because there aren't any more mortgage payments, which is the largest portion of your overall monthly expense.

> ***If you don't have time to wait to earn an income, a PPI may be a better investment instead of rentals.***

Wholesaling and fix and flip projects can provide a more immediate income but there is no long-term growth associated with these strategies. The big difference between PPIs and these two strategies is that there is a lot more work involved in these, so they aren't passive investments. If you don't have much free time to work on these strategies, these are not good strategies for you. Also, fix and flips are a lot riskier than PPIs.

PPIs, on the other hand, are always 100% passive. You invest your money and you start to receive your interest payments, usually every quarter, and you don't have to lift a finger after you make your initial investment. You don't even have to go to the bank since most PPIs are setup to deposit your payment directly into your bank account.

PPIs versus Private Mortgage Investments (PMIs)

The biggest difference between PPIs and PMIs is that a PMI is not very scalable or repeatable. This means that the more money you make, the more you will need to reinvest, and the harder it will be to find borrowers looking for these larger amounts to borrow. Most private placement investments can accept investments of $1M or even more if you want. Now, I would definitely recommend a better diversification strategy, but it is still feasible.

The other disadvantage with PMIs is that you are always dealing with a new borrower, in most cases, so you have no idea what you are getting into. Once you are working with an Exempt Market Dealer, you will be able to continue working with them for as long as you want to invest and for as long as they have new projects.

Working with a couple of proven credible EMDs could very well lead to you having more exposure to new reinvestment opportunities. Another disadvantage of investing in PMIs is that your money may very well be sitting around while your mortgage broker finds another private mortgage for you to invest in.

> ***During that time, your money is not earning interest so it reduces your overall return.***

For example, assume you make 12% for one year on a private mortgage investment but then it takes another 6 months to find you another investment. Your overall return is now 12% / 18 months = 8% annually, which is actually, less than most PPIs.

PPIs versus Mortgage Investment Corporations (MICs)

The difference between PPIs and MICs is that PPIs invest in only one project and MICs invest in several mortgages. Both investments are 100% passive and provide regular payments. Some MICs will pay monthly while others may pay quarterly. Both of these investments are usually RRSP eligible and accept cash.

> ***The biggest difference between a PPI and a MIC is that MICs provide returns less than what a PPI can provide.***

MICs generally pay about 5% return, while PPIs pay approximately 8% - 10% return. The reason for this big difference is because of the investment mix within a MIC. A MIC spreads its funds across several different investments at various returns. There is also a management fee charged within a MIC. In contrast, there is no fee with a PPI.

The other advantage of a PPI is that you get to choose the project you want to invest in. If you do not like a particular PPI project, you do not have to invest in it. With a MIC, you have no control over what your funds are being invested into. When you invest in a MIC, you are investing in the fund and not in any actual property.

Some MICs are publicly traded and can be bought and sold like stocks. Hence, they are highly liquid. PPIs, on the other hand, are investing in one project and you are locked in for the life of the project.

PPIs versus Real Estate Investment Trusts (REITs)

A REIT invests in multiple real estate projects. A REIT will own several properties. Their investments are usually large properties, such as large apartment buildings, hotels, hospitals or shopping malls. A REIT is bought and sold in units/shares like stocks and bonds. Similar to MICs, REITs can be bought and sold on the stock market, making them a very liquid investment.

> ***When you invest in a REIT, you are actually investing in the fund and not a property. Your return is based on the ability of the REIT fund manager.***

A typical REIT provides a return that is usually quite a bit less than the average PPI.

In conclusion, there are many different types of *passive* real estate investment options each with their own advantages and disadvantages. In my opinion, Private Placement Investments are the best overall passive investment alternative.

CHAPTER 9

Passive Investment Planning

Most people spend more time planning a special dinner event then they do planning their own investment strategy. Part of the reason is that they have never been shown how to invest before. Another reason is that they have never had to know how to invest, or so they thought.

People have left their investment planning in the hands of their investment advisors who can end up investing those funds into bad performing investments such as mutual funds, bonds, etc. The investment advisor's justification is that they think that the best way to protect their clients' investments is by sticking to 'conservative investments'.

People need to take control of their investments and develop an investment plan that is aligned with their goals. You don't want a plan that is contradictory to your goals. Unfortunately, I see it all the time in real estate investing. People are investing in a specific real estate investment strategy because someone told them they should. They don't even understand what their investment goals are.

There are a number of factors to consider when defining your goals and deciding what activities, you should perform to achieve these goals. Here are a few of the more common factors that have to be considered when creating your investment plan.

Age - Age will determine how much time you have to meet your retirement goals. This, together with your current savings, will determine how much you have to save and earn to retire. The older you are the more you may have to save if you don't already have a lot of savings.

Current Savings - How much savings do you currently have on deposit to invest with? The more you have saved, the less you will need to save to reach the same goals. If you are starting with $100,000, you will have to save a lot more than if you are starting with $500,000 with the same goal in mind.

Income Requirements - What is the income that you require to be able to quit your day job or to live comfortably when you retire? If you are investing to replace your income, you need to know how much you will need to be earning from your investments in order to make that happen.

Risk Tolerance - How much risk can you tolerate? Age will also be a contributing factor to this characteristic. If you are risk-averse, then you want to stick to low-risk investments such as private placement investments. If you have a higher risk tolerance, then maybe you can consider investing in fix and flips for short-term cash.

Income Sources - Do you have other income sources, such as a day job, and how important is it for your investments to provide a good return? For example, do you have other income from a job that you love and therefore, you are only seeking investments to merely supplement rather than replace your income altogether?

Other Investments - How much money do you have invested in other investments and how do those fit into your overall plan and strategy? Perhaps you already have some passive investments and you are now able to take part in investments that are a bit riskier.

Finally, your investment goals need to be SMART goals. These are goals that are specific, measurable, attainable, realistic and time-based.

9.1 - Investment Goals

Before you start investing, it's important to understand what your goals are. Most people start investing without engaging in any type of goal setting whatsoever. They have not taken control of their investments. This approach can be quite problematic.

Without goals, when will you know you have reached your intended result? There are many books written on goal setting but the fundamental premise is that "to be successful, you need to have goals". Also, your goals need to be written down.

A goal that is not written down is just an idea or a wish.

There are some basic characteristics of goals that need to be followed when defining and setting your goals.

You need to define SMART goals. I have seen SMART stand for several different things. The version of the acronym I like to use is Specific, Measurable, Achievable, Relevant and Time-based. Let me expand on each of these.

Specific

To be effective, your investment goals need to be specific. Merely saying you want to make a lot of money is not being very specific. Just saying that you want to make $1M is also not that specific. The other problem with just saying you want to make $1M is that there is some psychological power that is often attached to it.

Most people when asked how much money they want to make, save, earn or have, always like to give out $1M as an answer, implying there's some magical feeling attached to that number.

Having a goal, that says you want to *earn $100,000 this year and save 10% of your earnings and invest that money into a private equity with Company A* is an example of a specific goal. It's specific and it's also time-based, which is another important characteristic.

Measurable

A goal should be measurable. For example, when you say you are going to lose 10 pounds in three months, you can jump on a scale at any point in time and see if you have lost that amount of weight, or where you are in the process. The scale, in this case, is your measuring device and lets you know how you are progressing.

Using our previous investment example, if you decide that your investment goal is to earn $100,000 this year and save 10% of your earnings while investing that money into a private placement investment with Company A, you should have no problem measuring that goal. You should also be able to see how much money you have saved each month and if you have enough money to invest.

Achievable

There are some mixed views on how realistic and achievable your goals should be. Some experts say that you should have really big goals. That way, if you don't reach your goals, you have still achieved something significant.

For example, let's say you set a goal of wanting to save $50,000 while earning a salary of only $100,000. That's quite a stretch. Consequently, if you end up only saving $30,000, that's still pretty good because you initially set the bar high.

Other experts say that if you set goals too high, you will become disappointed and give up altogether. In this example, you may see that you have only saved $2,500 after two months and realize there's no way you can reach $50,000 in 12 months, causing you to give up altogether. This is a very common theme when it comes to weight loss goals.

Personally, I believe you should set goals that are just beyond a comfortable reach so that it forces you to extend yourself just a little. For example, let's say you know you can save $10,000 per year since you have been doing it for a couple of years. However, this year, you have received a raise, so now you set a goal to save $20,000 per year but you end up only saving $15,000. That's still more than your previous amount of $10,000 even though you didn't reach the $20,000 goal.

> ***Goals need to be a little challenging but not so painful that they are demotivating.***

Relevant

Goals need to be relevant.

You don't want to set a goal of owning rental properties if you are looking to supplement your income in the short-term. People think that they will be able to have enough net income from the difference between their expenses and their rental income. As I have said many times before, this is the biggest lie in real estate. Rental properties are a long-term investment strategy that requires you to hold onto properties for at least 10 years before you can actually earn an income from those properties. Also, don't forget the management associated with owning those rental properties can take up a lot of your time and may cost you money.

Let's say you have $200,000 and you want to buy some real estate in order to replace your current income. So, you end up buying a 4-plex for $800,000. As a result, you need about $176,000 to purchase the property because the banks want you to put up 20% in addition to paying for closing costs. In addition, of course, you also have to qualify for a mortgage.

Your rental income is $1,500 per unit, which amounts to a total of $6,000 a month while your monthly expenses are $5,400 a month. This means you now currently have $600 a month in positive cash flow or $7,200 a year. However, this is not very passive and, believe me, it only takes one tenant to eat up that cash flow. I had one tenant recently that cost me $30,000 to get him out.

If your objective is to earn an income, a more relevant goal would be to invest that $200,000 in a private placement investment and earn 10% per year. That's an almost guaranteed $20,000 a year in contrast to your rental income which is contingent on a reliable tenant. Furthermore, instead of getting a mortgage, you can take out a Home Equity Line of Credit (HELOC) on your existing home, and invest another $200,000 in your income generating private placement investment. Now, you are earning $40,000 (minus your mortgage loan costs) a year for doing nothing, and now your investments are aligned with your goals.

Time-Based

You need to set hard dates for your investment goals and make sure you meet those dates. If you have a goal of saving $12,000 in one year and you have saved $5,000 and you only have 6 months left, you need to increase your savings for the next 6 months. This means you would have to save $1,167 per month, on average. So maybe you eat out less, buy fewer clothes, forego a few more extravagances or find some other way to generate more income.

You could even state your goal to be that you want to save $1,000 a month for the next 12 months for a total of $12,000 and then you would invest those savings in a private placement investment. Now you have a monthly goal and a yearly goal.

The problem with yearly goals is people tend to start adjusting and trading between months. Maybe they only save $500 one month but then tell themselves they are going to save $1,500 the next month only to find out they are not able to do so. Then they get frustrated and start abandoning their goals.

In summary, in order to have a good investment strategy, it's important to set SMART goals and to stick to them.

9.2 - How to Develop an Investment Plan

Once you have defined your investment goals, you will need to develop a sound investment plan. A good investment plan needs to be as detailed as possible and needs to address all of your investment goals. Once you have developed a plan, you need to execute it as if your life depended on it. In a lot of cases, an investment plan generally consists of a retirement plan within it. So, in essence, your life does literally depend on it.

Most people today do not have an investment plan, let alone any savings plan, so they have no idea how they are going to retire. I meet people all the time who are in their 60s and 70s and are still working. They are still trying to retire, yet they have no plan. Some are looking for the secret "get rich quick" scheme. Or worse, they aren't really looking at all. The joke is that they see themselves working right up until noon on the day of their funeral.

Let's assume you have the following goals as part of your overall investment plan:

1. Retire at age 65 with an annual income of $100,000 per year.
2. Save 12% of your annual income of $100,000 for your retirement.
3. Invest in Private Placement Investments.
4. Earn a minimum of 10% return each year with your investments.

Let's also assume you are starting with an existing savings of $100,000.

Therefore, a list of activities in your plan might look like this:

1. Set up an investment account.
2. Deposit the $100,000 into your account.
3. Set up an automated bank-transfer of $1,000 to be transferred every month from your personal account to your investment account.
4. Develop a budget that covers all of your expenses.

5. If your income minus your expenses is less than $1,000, look for ways to reduce your expenses.
6. Reduce your spending as identified above.
7. Obtain a list of Exempt Market Dealers and their associated projects.
8. Evaluate the Private Placement Investment projects against the criteria we identified previously.
9. Select one or two Private Placement Investment projects.
10. Contact the EMD and open an account with them.
11. Invest your first $100,000 in one or two projects.
12. At maturity, say in two years, reinvest your profits into your next project.
13. Continue reinvesting until $1,000,000 has been accumulated.
14. Once you have earned $1,000,000, you should be able to retire and earn $100,000 per year by investing in similar projects at 10%.

There you have it. A simple plan. Now, let's see how all this calculates out.

Assumptions

Investment Term: 2 Years
Initial investment: $100,000
Annual Contribution: 12%, which is $12,000 every year, or $24,000 every 2 years.
Interest Rate: 10% per year, or 20% every 2 years.
Marginal Tax Rate: 40%
Starting Age: 40

Age	Investment	Return	Taxes	After Tax	New Contr.	Balance
40	$100,000	$20,000	$8,000	$12,000	$24,000	$136,000
42	$136,000	$27,200	$10,880	$16,320	$24,000	$176,320
44	$176,320	$35,264	$14,106	$21,158	$24,000	$221,478
46	$221,478	$44,296	$17,718	$26,577	$24,000	$272,056
48	$272,056	$54,411	$21,764	$32,647	$24,000	$328,703
50	$328,703	$65,741	$26,296	$39,444	$24,000	$392,147
52	$392,147	$78,429	$31,372	$47,058	$24,000	$463,204
54	$463,204	$92,641	$37,056	$55,585	$24,000	$542,789
56	$542,789	$108,558	$43,423	$65,135	$24,000	$631,924
58	$631,924	$126,385	$50,554	$75,831	$24,000	$731,754
60	$731,754	$146,351	$58,540	$87,811	$24,000	$843,565
62	$843,565	$168,713	$67,485	$101,228	$24,000	$968,793
64	$968,793	$193,759	$77,503	$116,255	$24,000	$1,109,048

Now, this plan shows that if you start at 40, with an initial investment of $100,000, and continue to contribute $24,000 every two years and reinvest your earnings, you will have grown your investment portfolio to over $1M by the time you are 65.

You could now invest that amount at an average return of 10% and receive an interest income of over $100,000 per year without ever having to work again. You are now ready to retire.

Here's an example of what happens if you start 5 years later, at only 45, and want to achieve the same results. What kind of contribution would you need to make in order to achieve the same results as the prior illustration? Again, assume you are starting with an initial investment of $100,000:

Age	Investment	Return	Taxes	After Tax	Contr.	Balance
45	$100,000	$20,000	$8,000	$12,000	$28,000	$140,000
47	$140,000	$28,000	$11,200	$16,800	$28,000	$184,800
49	$184,800	$36,960	$14,784	$22,176	$28,000	$234,976
51	$234,976	$46,995	$18,798	$28,197	$28,000	$291,173
53	$291,173	$58,235	$23,294	$34,941	$28,000	$354,114
55	$354,114	$70,823	$28,329	$42,494	$28,000	$424,608
57	$424,608	$84,922	$33,969	$50,953	$28,000	$503,560
59	$503,560	$100,712	$40,285	$60,427	$28,000	$591,988
61	$591,988	$118,398	$47,359	$71,039	$28,000	$691,026
63	$691,026	$138,205	$55,282	$82,923	$28,000	$801,949
65	$801,949	$160,390	$64,156	$96,234	$28,000	$926,183

In this example, you see that the contribution would now have to be at least $28,000 every two years, which is $14,000 per year. That's an extra $2,000 per year that you would have to save if you are starting at age 45 instead of at age 40. And you didn't even reach $1M in the second example. The earlier you start your investment plan, the easier it will be to accumulate the earnings you require to be able to retire comfortably and to do the things you want to do in the meantime.

If you had started this program at age 25, with only $2,000 in savings, you would only have had to contribute $500 a month for the next 40 years to accumulate $1M by age 65.

These examples assume that this is a *cash* investment and does not look at the benefits of investing through a registered account of RRSPs or TFSAs. The magic of compounding inside your registered account makes your goal of achieving $1M by retirement much more realistic.

For example, if you started your plan at age 45, with $100,000 in your RRSP and only contributed $500 per month back into your RRSP for the next 20 years, you could achieve your goal of $1M by age 65.

Age	Investment	Return	Taxes	After Tax	Contr.	Balance
45	$100,000	$20,000	$0	$20,000	$12,000	$132,000
47	$132,000	$28,000	$0	$26,400	$12,000	$170,400
49	$170,400	$36,960	$0	$34,080	$12,000	$216,480
51	$216,480	$46,995	$0	$43,296	$12,000	$271,776
53	$271,776	$58,235	$0	$54,355	$12,000	$338,131
55	$338,131	$70,823	$0	$67,626	$12,000	$417,757
57	$417,757	$84,922	$0	$83,551	$12,000	$513,309
59	$513,309	$100,712	$0	$102,662	$12,000	$627,971
61	$627,971	$118,398	$0	$125,594	$12,000	$765,565
63	$765,565	$138,205	$0	$153,113	$12,000	$930,678
65	$930,678	$160,390	$0	$186,136	$12,000	$1,128,813

In conclusion, it's important to know what your investment goals are and to develop a plan that will help you achieve those goals. You have to make sure that the activities defined in your investment plan are specifically aligned with your investment goals and that they are not conflicting.

Finally, all you have to do is execute that plan with the utmost discipline.

Well defined goals, together with a well thought out plan where the activities are executed without any question, is the ultimate secret to success.

9.3 - The Secret to Diversification

One way to reduce the risk of your investments is by diversifying. Or is it?

To diversify your investments means to spread your investment portfolio across several different investments. To most investment advisers, this means putting your money into different stocks and different mutual funds. The problem with that type of diversification is that it's still the same asset class. All your money is still invested in just stocks and bonds.

Real estate investing brings another level of diversification by bringing in a whole different asset class, especially when using Private Placement Investments.

The reason why people want to diversify is so that they aren't "putting all their eggs in one basket". However, a 'stock-only' diversification strategy means investing in stocks in different sectors. For example, some stocks are in oil and gas companies, some stocks are in financial companies and some stocks are in technology companies. Your portfolio appears to be diversified. Regardless, it's still ALL stocks.

Real estate brings another level of diversification since you are exposing yourself to a totally different asset class. As shown earlier, there are many ways you can invest in real estate.

Investing in *multiple* real estate investment strategies is another way you can diversify *within* the real estate asset class. For example, you could own some rental properties, you could invest in a couple of fix and flips and you could invest in some mortgage-based investments. However, this means you have to become an expert in each of these strategies, which is not something most people want to do.

Just like stock investing there are many things to know about when investing in real estate and choosing the right real estate mix for your portfolio.

Income vs Equity

Some real estate investment strategies are more designed to provide an immediate cash return/income, while others are more geared towards long term equity growth.

For example, purchasing a property with the intent of fixing it up and selling it right away for a profit, is a short-term cash return and is an example of an income solution.

Purchasing a 4-unit building and renting it out does not provide any short term income and really only starts making you money after 10 years or more. However, during those 10 years, the property is appreciating and the mortgage is being paid down. Thus, the equity in your investment property is building up over time. You will only make your money when you sell or refinance after 10 years or more.

Long Term vs Short Term

Some investments are short-term while others are long-term. In the above examples, the fix and flip investment is a short-term investment strategy while the buy, rent and hold investment is a much longer-term strategy. Private placement investments are medium-term and are generally 2 to 5 years.

Therefore, if you don't need money right away, buy rent and hold might be a better option for you or maybe private placement investments. As already shown, there are several other real estate investment strategies, all providing short or long-term returns.

Return on Investment

The return on investment depends on the type of investment and the risk associated with that investment.

For example, investing in private mortgages with a loan to value (LTV) of 80% may only pay 10% per year on the money loaned. Another second mortgage investment with a higher LTV, of say 90%, may pay 15% per year. The 90% LTV is a higher risk investment because there may not be enough money left over to pay out all of the mortgages if the property ever has to be sold for whatever reason. Private placement investments can provide a return on investment of between 8% to 10%, and sometimes higher.

Risk vs Reward

The different investment strategies provide different risk/reward profiles which, as a result, pay different rates of return.

For example, fix and flips are probably the riskiest investment and investors could make as high as a 50% return on their investments. Private mortgage investments and private placement investments may only pay a 10% return per year and are very conservative with low risk. Lease Option investments may pay a good return of 15% per year and are generally medium risk and medium term.

Age of Investor

Your age will also influence your investment strategy and the diversification choices that you make.

For example, if you are 30 years old, you can afford to invest in some strategies that are a bit riskier. If the investment fails, you have more time to recover and to earn back your losses. If you are 70, you probably want to invest in more conservative investments, such as private placement investments, since you might be depending on that money as a form of income and it would be very hard for you to replace the money should you lose it in any investment.

"Put all your eggs in one basket and then watch the basket"

— Andrew Carnegie

One way to diversify within real estate, and to keep your risk relatively low, is to become an expert in one real estate investment strategy and then to invest in multiple projects within that strategy.

This is much different than a stock-based diversification strategy where you are only investing in stocks. With stock-based diversification, you are investing with many different companies that you would have to subsequently spend a lot of time researching.

A real estate based diversification strategy only works when you have found one investment strategy that you are happy with and you invest in multiple projects within this strategy. However, you continue to watch your "basket" on all your investment projects.

For example, let says you chose Private Placement Investments as your real estate investment strategy. By the way, this should be your number one strategy if you are looking for a passive investment that provides immediate and ongoing income.

What you would do then is find a good Exempt Market Dealer. You research the projects that they have available and you invest some money into a specific project. Six months later you invest in another project and you keep repeating this strategy until your money runs out.

Now you have money invested in several different projects with the same Exempt Market Dealer but you are diversified across several different projects. Each of the projects will be maturing at different times so you can also line up any additional monies you want to add to the balance of your investment. Your portfolio would look something like this.

Let's say you have $400K to invest:

Month 0: Project A: $100K

Month 6: Project B: $100K

Month 12: Project C: $100K

Month 18: Project D: $100K

Month 24: Project E: $120K (reinvest proceeds from Project A)

Month 30: Project F: $120K (reinvest proceeds from Project B)

Month 36: Project G: $120K (reinvest proceeds from Project C)

Month 42: Project H: $120K (reinvest proceeds from Project D)

This strategy is simple to implement and simple to monitor. It also limits your exposure by spreading your money across multiple projects. A good Exempt Market Dealer advisor will be able to implement this strategy for you.

In conclusion, the key when investing in real estate is to take all of the factors into consideration and figure out which investment strategy makes the most sense for you based on these factors, and finally follow that one investment strategy. I would not recommend trying to use more than one strategy, especially if you are looking for a passive investment strategy. The exception to this rule is if you plan on becoming a full-time investor.

CHAPTER 10

Next Steps

The real key to making money in real estate investing it to get started as soon as possible and to invest as quickly as possible. Many people spend way too much time analyzing a particular real estate deal, which is strange since they had not spent any time analyzing their mutual fund investments in the past.

A contributing factor to this acquired behavior is that they lost a bunch of money in the stock market so now they are 'investment shy' and are very reluctant to go into another investment of any kind without doing a proper analysis.

Real estate is one of those unknowns for most people. In addition, there are a lot of stories out there about the "horrors" of owning real estate. This is one of the reasons I am focused on passive real estate investment strategies using private placement investments.

Now, I'm not saying that you shouldn't do your own investigation and analysis. It's equally important that you don't take *forever* to analyze the projects. I have had people take so long to analyze their investment, that their investment actually lost 1% to 2%, and sometimes even more because they took so long and their money was just sitting there doing nothing. Don't get caught up in analysis-paralysis!

Time is money. If you take too long to invest, you will reduce your overall return on your money.

For example, let's say you are considering investing in a private placement investment. You decide you want to invest $100,000 and you are looking to get a 12% return on your investment, which is 1% per month or $1,000 per month.

Now, let's say you get busy and you don't invest right away. And let's say you also spend a lot of time analyzing the deal. As a result, you end up only investing after two months. Meanwhile, your money was sitting in a cash account and not earning any interest. Your delays actually cost you 2%, or $2,000. So, the actual return on your investment, when you do invest, is now only 10% because for 2 months your investment earned $0.

Money needs to be moving in order to make money. Money needs to be invested to make money.

Another problem I see is people being overprotective of their money by only investing only a portion of it.

For example, I had this one guy tell me how well a particular investment was doing. He had made a 20% return on the investment. I asked him how much he had invested. He said he had about $100,000 in this particular investment. So, I asked him how big his portfolio was and what were his other investments. He told me he had sold off his other investments and that he had about $900,000 sitting in a cash account, which was earning 0%. I then explained to him that his investment actually only made 2%, since it represented the overall return of his entire portfolio.

As a result of his fears, he ended up just keeping up with inflation. He had no other investments. He didn't even have a plan. He didn't even have any diversification strategy, let alone a compounding strategy.

It's important to get educated fast, invest in the right investments and then get your money working as quickly as possible.

10.1- How to Start Investing in Private Placement Investments

Starting to invest in Private Placement Investments is easy but you want to make sure you are investing with the right Exempt Market Dealer. There are many companies offering private placement investments.

The first thing you need to do when deciding to invest in private placement investments is to decide on your goals. Private placement investments can provide consistent returns over a specified period. If your goal is to start with an initial investment of say, $100,000 and turn it into $600,000 over ten years, by leveraging the tax savings from your RRSP, then a private placement investment is right for you. If you are looking for a higher return and are willing to take on bigger risks and you have lots of time to fail, then PPIs may not be the best thing for you. The key characteristics of a PPI are consistency, higher returns, low risk, scalable, repeatable and very passive.

So, if you decided that PPIs are the investment strategy of choice for your investment goals, then you need to start looking for an Exempt Market Dealer. While there are many Exempt Market Dealers out there, you have to make sure you do your due diligence. That's a good thing and a bad thing.

The good thing is that you should be able to easily find all the Exempt Market Dealers and all the terms and provisions of their respective PPI projects, so it won't.be that hard to evaluate each of them. The bad thing is that because there are so many it could be a lot of work and it might be difficult to choose.

In addition to the criteria described earlier, when looking at Exempt Market Dealers and their associated projects, you want to make sure that you base your evaluations on some basic principles:

A good PPI must:

- Provide higher returns. Most good PPIs provide between 8% to 12% return, depending on the size and term of the project.
- Are involved in Real Estate. I prefer to invest in PPIs that are focused on real estate only.
- Allow multiple sources of funds. All PPIs that I have worked with allow cash investments as well as registered funds, such as RRSPs.
- Have a proven track record by the company and its owners. You must investigate the company and the owners of the company to see how successful they have been in the past and if they have had any trouble paying their investors.
- Be scalable and repeatable. The more money you make, the more money you will have to reinvest. The bigger the amount, the more you want to be able to invest your money. You also want to be able to find your next investment without having to spend a lot of time looking around for it, while your money sits idle.

Once you find the Exempt Market Dealer you want to invest in, find a good advisor to work with.

Most Exempt Market Dealers have many advisors working for them and so all you have to do is search for the Exempt Market Dealer name and you should be able to come up with a list of PPI advisors for that PPI.

It could also be that you learn about the Exempt Market Dealer by first contacting a PPI Advisor and that's OK too. Just beware, that you aren't pushed into investing in one of their PPI products without first doing your proper due diligence.

Once you have selected an Exempt Market Dealer and you are working with an advisor you now want to look at the actual PPIs. Keep in mind, these products need to be aligned with your goals. At the same token, you always want to think about diversifying your portfolio. Perhaps you might decide to invest in multiple products at the start, or you wait for 6 months and invest in a second PPI at that time. Either way, I would recommend investing in multiple PPIs to minimize your risk and optimize your compounding strategy, which is very effective inside your RRSP.

Next, you should select one or two PPIs that you want to invest in. If your available funds were $100,000 or less, I would recommend you go with only one PPI so you do not have to learn about too many PPIs too soon.

The next step is deciding how you will fund the investment and open up the appropriate account. If you are investing in cash, that is easy. All you have to do is write a cheque for the amount of the investment. If you are investing with an RRSP or another type of registered account, then you will need to open a registered account with the Exempt Market Dealer you have selected.

Once the account has been set up, you will then either make a deposit or transfer your funds from another registered account into this new account. Your PPI Advisor will handle all of this for you.

The next step is to actually invest. This means actually directing the money from your newly setup account into the PPI that you have selected. This is a simple as filling out some necessary forms that will be provided to you by your advisor. Now there are many smaller steps within this step but a good advisor will be able to help you with all of these steps.

Finally, all you have to do you simply sit back and watch your investment grow. You will want to monitor the payments and growth every three months or so but that's the fun part! Imagine that you invested $100,000 in one project and then invested another $100,000 in another project. If the return on each of these investments is paying 10% per year, you will see your portfolio grow by about $5,000 every three months. It is pretty exciting to watch.

> ***Passive investing does not mean total abdication. You still want to monitor your portfolio and keep on top of it so that there are no surprises.***

If you are trying to accelerate your portfolio growth, you should also continue to save and make further contributions. The more money you invest now, the bigger your portfolio will grow and the more you will have when you really need it.

In conclusion, it is really quite easy to start investing in Private Placement Investments. You just have to make sure you find the right Exempt Market Dealer that provides the right products and work with the right advisor.

10.2 - How to Double Your Money in 8 Years

A lot of people think that the only benefit from an RRSP account is that it is used to reduce their taxes at the time of deposit. When you make a deposit into your RRSP account, it reduces your taxes that have to pay for the year in which you make that deposit. The amount of reduction is calculated based on your marginal tax rate at the time of your contribution.

For example, assume you earn $120,000 a year and your marginal income tax rate is 40%. Any contribution you make will reduce your taxable income by 40%. This means that if you make a deposit of say $25,000, you would reduce the tax you have to pay by $10,000.

There is a maximum allowable contribution and it is based on a percentage of your salary, up to a maximum of $26,010 as of 2017. People with an employee pension plan will not be able to contribute as much. An RRSP is one of the best tax benefits you can receive and you should always try to make the maximum allowable contribution each year. This is part of taking control of your financial planning.

The next step is where the real magic happens. Not only do you get a big tax reduction when you deposit money into your RRSP account, but the money inside your RRSP can also earn money interest tax-free until it is time to take that money out. Most people do not understand this and they don't understand the power of compounding to take advantage of the non-taxable income earned by your investments inside an RRSP.

For example, let's say you invest $100,000 of your RRSP into a private placement investment. And let's assume your investment earns a return of 10% per year and that the investment term is for 2 years.

After 2 years, your investment fund now has $120,000 in it. The original $100,000 plus the $20,000 it earned over the two years. If this same investment was made outside of your RRSP, your fund would only contain $112,000, because you would have had to pay $8,000 in income tax, again assuming your marginal tax rate of 40%.

The magic in the RRSP is that you now have $8,000 more to reinvest since the tax is deferred. Furthermore, this keeps happening every time your investment matures and you reinvest the full amount, which is every two years in our example. This is what the example looks like over 20 years.

Age	Investment	Return	Taxes	After Tax	Contr.	Balance
45	$100,000	$20,000	$0	$20,000		$120,000
47	$120,000	$24,000	$0	$24,000		$144,000
49	$144,000	$28,800	$0	$28,800		$172,800
51	$172,800	$34,560	$0	$34,560		$207,360
53	$207,360	$41,472	$0	$41,472		$248,832
55	$248,832	$49,766	$0	$49,766		$298,598
57	$298,598	$59,720	$0	$59,720		$358,318
59	$358,318	$71,664	$0	$71,664		$429,982
61	$429,982	$85,996	$0	$85,996		$515,978
63	$515,978	$103,196	$0	$103,196		$619,174

In this example, your $100,000 initial contribution will actually double in only 8 years to over $207,000. In 20 years, that one-time contribution grew to over $600,000. That's six times the original investment, without having to make any additional annual contribution — and all you had to do was find an investment that can support this strategy.

Real estate investing doesn't have to be difficult. There are only a few simple criteria that you need to follow for this type of return to occur.

The first is that you need to have the initial $100,000 to invest with. You also need room in your RRSP to allow you to top up your RRSP so you have a balance of $100,000 to start with. This shouldn't be a problem if you have been earning enough and if you do not have a defined pension plan. At the time of this writing, the maximum allowable annual contribution is $26,230. This would be reduced based on your defined employee pension plan.

The second thing you need to do is find a good passive investment strategy that will grow with you. In this example, the private placement investment must be paying 10% per year and has to mature after two years. At the time of maturity, there has to be another investment available that will allow you to reinvest at the same 10% and for the next two-year period. Furthermore, the investment vehicle has to be able to accept your increasing investment amounts.

In our example above, the initial investment was $100,000 in the first year. In year 20, the investment was over $600,000. There aren't a lot of other investments that can accommodate such a high investment amount with the type of security that Private Placement Investments can offer.

You should also make sure you diversify your investment by splitting it across two or more projects. Furthermore, you could even accelerate it so that you start another investment in one year. In this case, you have a reinvestment happening every year and you don't have to wait for two years to compound the entire amount.

The other thing you have to make sure of is that you start planning three months in advance of the maturity of each investment. You have to keep your money moving. If your money is sitting in a cash account, you reduce your returns.

People tell me all the time, about the great return they made on this particular investment, yet all their other investments had very poor returns. No one talks about the bad ones. The return you need to be focusing on is the return of your *entire* portfolio.

If you have a $1M portfolio and you have $500,000 invested at 10% and you have the other $500,000 only earning 2%, your overall return is 6%. And what happens if the other $500,000 was sitting in a cash account not earning anything? Your average return, in that case, would have only been 5%.

This may still be a good return for some people but it's something you need to be aware of when you are planning. You can make a much better return by diversifying your portfolio across a series of Private Placement Investments with alternating maturity dates.

What if your money sits around for 6 months while you look for the next investment? This happens when you have a bad investment advisor who isn't really paying attention to your portfolio. You should never have your money not earning at least 8% per year. This is a lot easier than you think with the right investment advisor.

The trick to long term investing is what I call 'conservative consistency'.

Invest regularly so that your money is always working and try to achieve an average return of at least 8% per year. This isn't going to happen with many stock market investments with most investment advisors.

The stock market is underperforming and has not been able to provide consistent results. If you are investing in mutual funds, these funds may also underperforming and some are charging high management fees.

A good investment advisor that specializes in Private Placement Investments should be able to help you with your overall investment strategy and help you to achieve the results shown in the above example. If you aren't earning a minimum return of 8% across your entire portfolio, then it's time to get a new investment advisor. Furthermore, if you aren't working with anyone, then it's important to find one and start taking control of your financial plans.

10.3 - How to Turn $100,000 into $600,000 in Just 10 Years

You may have jumped to this section right away because of the title. Everyone wants to know how to grow their portfolio fast. However, most people also want to ensure that their investment is secure. Let's look at a way to provide both a good return and a secure investment.

Yes, it is very possible to turn $100,000 into $600,000 in just 10 years. However, there are special ingredients required to do this.

First of all, you need the initial $100,000, to begin with. You need a strong base to start with and then build upon. Next, you have to be able to leverage the maximum contribution of your RRSP. That means you have to be able to make the maximum contribution allowable each year. You also need the room in your RRSP to be able to make the maximum contribution. At the time this book was written (2017), that maximum contribution is $26,230.

You also need an investment product that will accept RRSP funds and that pays at least a 10% return each year and that will mature in two years. If you have an investment that provides a higher return, it can take longer to mature.

This investment product must be consistent, scalable and repeatable. This means that the investment product must be able to provide consistent returns over the next 10 years. It must also be able to accept increasingly larger investments as your portfolio grows. Also, it must have new projects to invest in when the time comes to reinvest your monies at the time of maturity of your previous investment.

The most likely investment product that I am recommending is a Private Placement Investment. A good Private Placement Investment will provide a 10% annual return. A good PPI will usually accept larger amounts of investments. Some of the PPIs that I work with are raising $100M or more. Furthermore, it must be repeatable. Subsequently, most Exempt Market Dealers that I deal with continue to have new projects.

So, how can you start with a $100,000 and grow it to $600,000 in just under 10 years?

Step 1.

The first thing you need to do is find a good Private Placement Investment advisor to work with. This advisor has to be able to supply you with the PPI that will meet the qualifications previously mentioned. Also, the PPI needs to provide a 10% return. Furthermore, it must mature in two years and it must be repeatable and reusable.

Step 2.

Next, you want to sit down with your PPI Advisor and look at the projects that are available. A good PPI Advisor should have access to several projects at any one time — or at least know when the next project is coming up. Again, you are looking for a PPI that pays a return of at least 10% per year and has a term of two years, but no more than three years.

Step 3.

Once you decide which project you want to invest in, you will need to open up a registered account. Each Exempt Market Dealer is different, and each may use different Trustees to be the administrator for your RRSP account. The Trustee is the third party that oversees and administers the Self-Directed RRSP mortgage and handles the collection and distribution of payments between the borrower and you, the lender.

Step 4.

Next, you need to either deposit the money into that new account or transfer funds from an existing account to this new account. A good PPI Advisor will handle all the paperwork and do all this work for you. This should be as easy as possible for you.

Step 5.

Once the money has been transferred, then you want to invest your RRSP funds into that specific project you have already identified. At this point, you now have your first investment earning interest. Most PPIs will be paying the interest quarterly, so you would be able to see your investment growing every three months.

Step 6.

Next, you want to start making your maximum contribution to your new RRSP account. This can be done monthly or annually, as long as the additional funds are available for reinvestment for the next project.

Now, here's another bonus of investing through your RRSP. When you make your maximum annual contribution of $25,000 or more, you reduce your taxable income by the same amount. This means that if you have a marginal tax rate of 40%, it also reduces the amount of taxes you have to pay by $10,000. As a result, you would either reduce your taxes by $10,000 or you would get a refund of $10,000 if you are a salaried employee.

The net result is that it only costs you $15,000 to make a $25,000 deposit into your RRSP, and you get to invest the total $25,000 tax-free. Moreover, you can hang on to your $10,000 tax refund so you can deposit it into your RRSP the next year.

Step 7.

After two years, you cash out your investment and reinvest your original $100,000, plus the $20,000 that you earned in interest payments, plus the $50,000 you have saved through your regular contributions into another Private placement Investment.

Step 8.

Repeat steps 6 and 7 three more times for a total of 10 years.

So, here's what the numbers of this strategy look like.

Age	Investment	Return	Taxes	After Tax	Contr.	Balance
45	$100,000	$20,000	$0	$20,000	$50,000	$170,000
47	$170,000	$34,000	$0	$34,000	$50,000	$254,000
49	$254,000	$50,800	$0	$50,800	$50,000	$354,800
51	$354,800	$70,960	$0	$70,960	$50,000	$475,760
53	$475,760	$95,152	$0	$95,152	$50,000	$620,912
55	$620,912	$124,182	$0	$124,182	$50,000	$795,094
57	$795,094	$159,019	$0	$159,019	$50,000	$1,004,113
59	$1,004,113	$200,823	$0	$200,823	$50,000	$1,254,936
61	$1,254,936	$250,987	$0	$250,987	$50,000	$1,555,923
63	$1,555,923	$311,185	$0	$311,185	$50,000	$1,917,108
65	$1,917,108	$383,422	$0	$383,422	$50,000	$2,350,529

As you can see, the original investment was $100,000. The maximum contribution of $25,000 was made each year. I decided to use $25,000 just to make it more presentable and easier to understand in the table. The reinvestment term was two years.

At the end of the 10th year, the total accumulated amount was $620,912. What's even more interesting is that if you do this for only another 4 years you will accumulate over $1M. Continue until you are just over 65 and you will have over $2M. In addition, this is not taking into account the *increased* contribution limits that you can make if you want to take advantage of that. The results of this strategy are astounding. Real estate investing doesn't have to be hard or risky. *Conservative consistency* is all you need.

In conclusion, this is an easy way to turn $100,000 into $600,000 over a 10-year period. You also have to add an additional $150,000 investment over the same 10 years. That's a $15,000 annual contribution each year!

Conclusion

I want to thank you for taking the time to read this book. Most people are in trouble financially or need some type of direction for their investment planning. Now, more than ever, people are looking for investment and retirement solutions. The problem lies in the fact that most people don't know where to begin.

People gave up control of their investments or they never really took control of their investments.

The information in this book gives you all the tools you need to start taking control of your financial future and to start using real estate as a vehicle to create financial freedom. You don't have to win big with real estate. This is where most people go wrong when trying to invest in real estate. Real estate can be a simple solution and a simple investment strategy if done properly.

Passive real estate investing can provide simple consistent returns that will challenge most guaranteed investments.

Therefore, it is wise to start taking control of your investments. Start taking control of your financial future. Define your goals, put together a plan and start executing it.

Best of luck to you in your endeavors!

If you would like more information on our programs and how we might be able to help, check out the following website:

www.jimpellerin.com

www.ingramcontent.com/pod-product-compliance
Lightning Source LLC
LaVergne TN
LVHW090402210926
848480LV00002B/426
* 9 7 9 8 2 1 5 3 7 8 9 8 4 *